QUICK CA$H
06

A Guide to Raising Money during Life's Planned and Unplanned Changes

Richard E. Schell
Attorney at Law

SPHINX® PUBLISHING
AN IMPRINT OF SOURCEBOOKS, INC.®
NAPERVILLE, ILLINOIS
WWW.SPHINXLEGAL.COM

First Edition, 2004

Published by: **Sphinx® Publishing, An Imprint of Sourcebooks, Inc.®**

<u>Naperville Office</u>
P.O. Box 4410
Naperville, Illinois 60567-4410
630-961-3900
Fax: 630-961-2168
www.sourcebooks.com
www.SphinxLegal.com

This publication is designed to provide accurate and authoritative information in regard to the subject
matter covered. It is sold with the understanding that the publisher is not engaged in rendering legal,
accounting, or other professional service. If legal advice or other expert assistance is required, the services of a competent professional person should be sought.

From a Declaration of Principles Jointly Adopted by a Committee of the
American Bar Association and a Committee of Publishers and Associations

This product is not a substitute for legal advice.

Disclaimer required by Texas statutes.

Library of Congress Cataloging-in-Publication Data
Schell, Richard E.
   Quick cash : a guide to raising money during life's planned and unplanned
changes / by Richard E. Schell.-- 1st ed.
      p. cm.
   Includes index.
   ISBN 1-57248-385-7 (alk. paper)
   1. Finance, Personal. 2. Fund raising. I. Title.

   HG179.S2643 2004
   332.024--dc22
                                        2004028067

Printed and bound in the United States of America.
VP Paperback — 10 9 8 7 6 5 4 3 2 1

ACKNOWLEDGEMENTS

I would like to thank the many people who helped with this book. I am particularly grateful to my family: my late parent who first impressed upon me the importance of being able to raise cash quickly, my wife who was a constant source of inspiration, and for my mother-in-law who helped in a million ways. And no acknowledgement would be complete without thanking my son, Nathan, for his patience and understanding as well.

Finally, I would like to thank Dianne Wheeler and Mike Bowen at Sphinx Publishing for their enthusiasm and superb editorial assistance.

Contents

Introduction . . . . **ix**

Part I: Changing Times **1**

Chapter 1: Personal Transitions **3**
The Transitions That Choose You
The Transitions That You Choose

Part Two: Evaluating Your Need **19**

Chapter 2: Cash Flow and Budgeting **21**
The Importance of Cash Flow
Goal Setting
Evaluating the Plan
Basic Budget Analysis

Part Three: Raising Quick Cash. 35

Chapter 3: Ask For It 37
Family and Friends
Governmental Programs
WIC
Hot Lunch Program
Temporary Aid to Needy Families
Earned Income Credit
Charities
Food Banks
Travelers Aid

Chapter 4: Borrow It 57
Family and Friends
Banks and credit unions
Pawn Shops
Consumer Finance Companies
Life Insurance
401(k) Accounts
Brokerage Accounts
Pension Accounts
Cash Advances

Chapter 5: Sell It 97
Antiques and Collectibles
Online Sites
Brick and Mortar Auctions

Ads
Garage Sales
Stock & other securities
Traditional and Roth IRA Accounts
529 and Coverdell (Educational)
IRA Accounts
Internal Assets

Chapter 6: Earn It 137
Temping
Freelancing
Part-time Jobs & Overtime
Odd Jobs and Jobs that are Odd
Using Your Creativity and Talent
Become a Landlord

Chapter 7: Find It. 179
Judgments
Unclaimed Property
Buried Treasure

Part Four: Making the Right Decision 187

Chapter 8: Quick Cash Cautions 189
Payday loans
Scams
Car Title Loans
Loan Sharks

Bargain sales of
real estate and collectibles
Tax Refund Loans

Glossary. 199

Appendix A: Quick Exercises. 205

Appendix B: Resources 209

Appendix C: 50 Fast Ways to Raise Cash 217

Appendix D: What Not to Do 221

Appendix E: Collectible Checklists. 225

Index 229

About the Author. 237

Introduction

This book explores five basic strategies that might be the solution to your need to raise cash quickly. Those strategies are—

1   Ask for it
2   Borrow it or pawn something for it
3   Cash in or sell something for it
4   Earn it
5   Find lost or unclaimed cash

There are a million different ways these strategies can be combined into different options for raising cash. A chapter is devoted to each strategy. The material highlights the advantages and disadvantages of each strategy and gives you an idea of the commitment, both in time and energy that each method takes.

There is also a chapter that tells you what *not to do*. Any time you raise cash, there may be legal issues involved and the choices you make may have some dire legal consequences. Additionally, even though something may be legal, it may not be in *your* particular best interest to do it. Those matters are covered as well.

The purpose of this book is to get you thinking of ways you can raise cash quickly. To get you started, the book begins with some of the common transitions that could lead you to needing this book and to let you know that you are not alone. You do not need to feel panicked in you decision-making, nor do you need to believe that no one else has ever been in your shoes.

You have made the first step in getting your finances back in order. Now you can use the information in this book to evaluate what you need, decide what you need to do, and learn how to follow through and get back on track.

Part I
Changing Times

Personal Transitions

1

People often find themselves needing to raise cash because of changes in their lives that have altered their finances. The change may be the result of one large sudden event or many small ones. Whatever the case, the result is the same—a sudden need to raise cash.

This section provides an overview of several common situations that cause people to take action to raise cash. The rest of the book provides more general strategies that can be mixed and matched to provide a road map through an altered financial landscape.

TRANSITIONS THAT CHOOSE YOU

Raising cash during the events of life that you didn't plan, and maybe didn't want, presents a challenge. It's one thing to volunteer for the experience of having to raise cash quickly, it's quite another to get drafted for it. But, the key might be to look at it as an adventure in using and finding resources to help move through challenging periods into better times. The most important element to moving through unplanned transitions, such as divorce and job loss, is to make a plan and then keep on moving no matter what.

Job Loss

Although job transitions can certainly be planned and carried out successfully, this section focuses on the unexpected *job loss*. Many different strategies can be used effectively to raise cash during periods of job loss. *Unemployment compensation* is certainly one of the big ones. (see Chapter 3.)

Above all, the key is to take a small breath before gearing up for the full hunt for the next job. A job loss is a chance to really get your act together. In the middle of the pain, trauma, and stress, there is still much opportunity that can be seized. Gather your friends around for support and keep moving with an eye toward the future. Remember, a crucial resource for the next step could be former co-workers. You also want to keep a couple of points in mind when leaving a job.

Severance

Negotiating a *severance package* calls for a cool head and an eye to the future. Be sure to take a moment away from the stress of losing your job to look for benefits that can be seized out of the bad situation. You may be able to wring some very real financial and nonmonetary benefits from your former employer that can be used to improve your cash situation. For example, some severance packages can be as generous as paid health insurance and up to a year or two of paid compensation and outplacement benefits. The key is to focus on the outcome of moving through the disruption to a better place. Thus, however the process of the job ending was handled, it may be in your best interest not to burn any bridges.

Even if a severance package is not formally offered, ask if one is available. It's time to aggressively explore the possibilities for any benefits from the former employer that can help pave the way through this period.

Don't limit your thoughts to just cash when it comes to severance. For example, many community job centers require a membership fee that has to be paid before job searchers can use their facilities. A membership fee in one of these groups, other networking groups, or outplacement groups is money that can be freed up for other purposes. If the company offers formal *outplacement* benefits supplied through a company or firm, seize them quickly. Any free phone calls, postage, and resume services that do not have to be purchased is a real financial benefit.

If there are no formal outplacement benefits and you are parting on good terms, ask if you can make job-hunting calls from one of their unused offices.

Many former employees who want to freelance find their first and best client is their former employer. Chapter 6 covers this option in more detail. It is definitely one you should keep in the back of your mind. Just because companies do not want, need, or desire employees, does not mean they don't have plenty of work that needs to be done.

Settling Accounts with Your Employer

Good financial housekeeping with your former or soon-to-be former employer can also be a recipe for more cash. For example, if you have any bonuses that are owed to you, ask if you can get them early, even if it comes at a discount. A bonus check in hand is worth two checks in the mail. Also, any expense account receipts that you have not gotten around to filing need to be rushed through right now. This is an important *to do* item for any employee whose job may be ending, but it is an urgent item if the company may be headed toward bankruptcy. Think carefully to see if your employer owes you any back pay, awards, prizes of any sort, sick pay, vacation pay, personal days, holiday pay, etc.

Anyone who is thinking of leaving a job or thinks that perhaps their employer is thinking of getting rid of them, should also give careful thought to any outstanding 401(k) monies they have taken out. Generally speaking, employers will require 401(k) loans to be repaid if the employee is terminated or leaves to find another job. (For more information on borrowing against 401(k) assets or to see if you qualify for a pension cash out see Chapter 4.)

Divorce

Divorce is a time of many changes and changes bring the need for cash—sometimes quickly. Just as the emotional changes of a divorce are life altering and profound, so are the changes in family finances. The changes involved in creating two new households demand new supplies of cash as new household furnishings are required, rent deposits are made, and utilities are paid.

Strategies for raising cash during a divorce may have legal implications related to the divorce itself, so examining laws that govern divorce and the division of property that goes with it is necessary. State law generally controls division of property in a divorce.

Several states follow the rule of *community property*. In Arizona, California, Idaho, Louisiana, Nevada, New Mexico, Texas, Washington, and Wisconsin, the courts look at any property acquired during the marriage as marital property that can be divided in a 50-50 split. However, assets you owned *before* the marriage are usually not counted as community property.

The other states follow the rule of *equitable distribution*. How exactly the marital property or estate is divided will depend on the laws of the individual state. However, equitable division does not necessarily mean half. In addition, there are special rules and requirements involved in dividing 401(k) and pension benefits. (As a general rule, if you acquired property from an inheritance during the marriage, that property will not be subject to division during a divorce.)

During this time, it is particularly important to think through actions you might have to take to raise cash. If you have a lawyer representing you during the divorce, ask him or her for advice. Any financial actions taken during a divorce can have serious consequences. For example, often court orders are entered that forbid either party from selling *marital assets*. In addition, the decision of whether to borrow money for living expenses or seek temporary support can affect the final division of property during the divorce.

Alimony

You should definitely keep in mind two things about *alimony*. Number one, divorce laws are state and local in their nature. You may not receive any alimony at all. Second, the granting of alimony or support is not as common as it used to be. Years ago when most women did not work, it was fairly common for women to receive alimony. However, times have changed, and men are sometimes awarded support. But before you count on this as a source of cash, you should definitely check with your attorney to see how common an award of alimony is in your state. In addition, even if alimony is awarded, it may be limited to a temporary aid for getting back into the job market. Nevertheless, temporary support payments may be a crucial source of cash during a divorce.

Property Division

Selling marital property without a court's permission to raise cash during a divorce is not a very good idea. Only custody determinations about children cause as much storm and drama as deciding how property will be divided. These are likely to be contentious and difficult issues.

However, having said that, states follow various rules regarding the division of marital property. Under a pure community property system, all property of either spouse becomes marital property during the marriage. This means all of it becomes subject to division by the court upon divorce.

For the states that do not follow that rule, there are *marital* and *nonmarital assets*. A nonmarital asset is property that one of the spouses acquired by gift or inheritance that never became part of the property of the marriage.

Parties in a divorce should be careful of selling any property during the divorce without first consulting with their attorneys. (However, if you know for sure you have authorization to dispose of the property than the rest of this book may be quite helpful, especially Chapter 5.)

Death of Spouse

Losing a spouse or partner has many implications for change across many aspects of life. The personal adjustments and financial implications may change everything from the smallest to the biggest aspects of life. Losing a loved one is like being caught in an avalanche of emotions and changes that are often bewildering and confusing. This section covers specific steps for dealing with the loss of a loved one.

For immediate sources of cash, many people look to joint bank accounts or payable on death accounts A *joint account* is one in which the people who own the account hold a *joint tenancy*. This means that when one of them dies, the interest in the account passes to the other one without requiring any action by a court. A *payable on death* (POD) account is different in that the person who owns the account selects who will receive the balance of the account when he or she dies, but the beneficiary does not have access to the account while the account owner is alive.

Additional sources of cash may have to come from credit card advances or by borrowing from family and relatives on a temporary basis. (For some helpful hints on how to structure loans from friends and family see Chapter 4.)

Some lenders may be willing to loan you money with an inheritance as collateral. This may be a way for you to raise money quickly. All of the considerations that apply to any other kind of borrowing activity also apply to this strategy. If the loan carries risks, then the borrower is going to have to expect he or she may have to pay a high interest rate. (Anyone interested in this as an option should definitely look at Chapter 4.)

In addition to cash, the deceased person may have owned other assets that will pass to their beneficiaries immediately without requiring *probate*. Probate is the court process of resolving the affairs of someone who has died. Because some assets pass without the actions of a court, they are called *nonprobate assets*. Some examples include life insurance, joint bank accounts, government A or B bonds, pension plans, profit sharing plans, stock bonus plan, and Social Security benefits. The surviving spouse should also check the employee manual to see if any part of the decedent's salary is payable to the surviving party.

Assets that are probate assets require the court's approval before they may be sold. Be very cautious about selling anything that you may have been left until the estate is closed. Until the estate is finally wound up, there may be many issues that affect the legal ownership of the property.

Following is a quick checklist of items that are needed by the court and others after the death of a spouse.

Checklist of necessary documents:
- ❏ the will—if there is one
- ❏ the living trust—if there is one
- ❏ at least a dozen certified death certificates
- ❏ Social Security numbers for the spouse and children
- ❏ insurance policies
- ❏ military discharge
- ❏ marriage licenses
- ❏ any video or list of valuables for insurance purposes

(Chapter 3 contains information you need to know about benefits the government provides when a spouse dies. Additional information is provided for veteran benefits.)

TRANSITIONS THAT YOU CHOOSE

Sometimes there are so many good and exciting things happening in life that there isn't enough time and money to keep up with all of them at once. Starting a business, going back to school, and starting a family are all examples of times when a cash crunch may come from a bout of good fortune. This section focuses on some of the unique circumstances that apply to the transitions you choose.

Starting a Business

The decision to open a business can be a way to raise quick cash. This is an option that many people pursue every year. There is a paradox here. Growing a business requires cash, so you have to use the very resource you hope to create. Yet, many people do start a side business successfully as a way to raise cash quickly.

Although this book is not primarily a guide to raising cash for a business start-up, its approach and strategies may help provide the business owner with some resources for raising cash for his or her personal needs. Some readers may well have started a business only to discover that it needed far more cash than they thought it would. Suddenly, they find themselves looking for ways to raise cash for their personal expenses, so they have more resources to pour back into the business to keep it running.

Projecting how much cash will be needed cannot be emphasized enough in the planning process. Do not plan for good times. Plan for especially bad times. If the norm in the industry that you are starting a business is that the start-up business loses money for the first year, plan to lose money for two years. Also, have back-up plans and then back up those plans so you can raise cash and raise it easily if you need to. If you have the thought you might ever start your own business, you should pay very close attention to Chapter 2 on budgeting and managing cash flow. (An ounce of proper prior planning could be worth a pound of cash raising later.)

Going Back to School

Going back to school on a full-time or part-time basis can bring many changes that might require some quick cash. These transitions can be especially hard for the person who is returning to school after having been a full-time employee. While it definitely pays to budget, it also pays to have back-up plans.

Universities do a very good job of covering financial aid sources such as loans. Many colleges have little-known-about loan programs for students who need to borrow a small amount of money in a hurry. A trip to the financial aid office is definitely worth making. If they do not administer the emergency loan program on campus, they should certainly know which office does. That office can supply the specific details about what to do to apply.

It pays to know all of the programs that the financial aid office has available. Many universities offer work-study and emergency loan programs, as well as student teaching, research, and administrative assistantships that can provide both tuition waivers and sometimes direct cash payments. Knowing your options before the cash is urgently needed will pay off in the long run.

When it comes to borrowing money, college students are placed in a particularly challenging position. Many of the borrowing strategies related to borrowing against major assets, like a house, may not work because they have no assets to borrow against. However, that does not mean there are not other options available.

College students often have lots of things they can sell. CDs are definitely a resale item with great potential through pawnshops or online. Furthermore, when cash is short, creativity had better be prepared to stand tall. For example, college is a place where almost any skill can be bartered for services or where the skill can be sold directly for cash. Always think of your need for quick cash in terms of what the ultimate benefit of getting the money will be. Few places lend themselves to bartering more readily to trading goods and services to avoid the need for cash than colleges. The students in writing classes need typing and proofing assistance. English majors enduring calculus may need tutoring. So if you have the calculus skills, you may be able to trade them for what you need.

In addition, colleges have supplied the impetus for several different enterprises ranging from movers and painters to maintenance services. Some enterprising students have also started video rental businesses. The list of services that can be sold or bartered to raise cash can be extensive.

Options for raising cash for college are not just limited to earning cash. If you have an IRA, you could possibly tap into it for educational expenses without penalty. If you make withdrawals from your individual retirement account and you use the money to pay for you, your spouse, child, or grandchild to go to an educational facility that is qualified by the IRS, then you still have to pay taxes on the money you take out, but you can avoid the 10% early withdrawal tax that the IRS would ordinarily charge. (This rule also applies to Roth IRAs.)

There are some restrictions. The money can only be used for *qualified higher education expenses*, which means it can be spent on tuition, fees, books, supplies, and equipment. Room and board counts if the student is at least part-time.

For more information on using an IRA for qualified educational expenses go to **www.irs.gov** and read *Notice 97-60, Using IRA Withdrawals to Pay Higher Education Expenses.*

An interesting new way to pay for college is through a program called *My Rich Uncle*. This is a novel concept in paying for college where students assign a percentage of their income after graduation in return for money up front in college. The website is at **www.myrichuncle.com**. Students agree to pay a fixed percentage of their income back after graduation, in return for financial assistance while in college. The idea is that as income goes up the value of the percentage goes up.

Many strategies in this book, such as loans or gifts, have very clear legal guidelines and rules. This one is so new that anyone contemplating this as a strategy should definitely consult with an attorney to review the agreement and its implications before signing on.

Retirement

Retirement is a time of change and changes can require quick cash. Many of the resources on part-time work and freelancing in Chapter 6 are helpful for these kinds of explorations. Retirees who want to raise cash should pay particular attention to the section on reverse mortgages in Chapter 4. If the retiree's house is paid for or has high equity, this can definitely be an option for raising cash. (It is one of the options that has a minimum age requirement of sixty-two, so it is definitely an option for *some* retirees.)

Getting Married

Getting married or *partnering* with a special someone is a very exciting time. It's also a time to explore creatively raising cash quickly. Many of the strategies in this book could definitely be used to raise cash quickly for this event. Certainly the planning exercises are key. With a wedding it may be helpful to focus on the end results and work backwards. Some creative couples even sign up sponsors and are quite successful in trading services for a mention in the program or tasteful display card. The website **www.theknot.com** has resources on various aspects of financing a wedding from budgeting to borrowing.

Several of the strategies that appear later in the book can also be used successfully to raise money for a wedding. For example, home equity loans, loans from family, and cash advances are certainly options to be considered.

Starting a Family

Having a baby means many different transitions. But transition periods can be times to raise cash by getting rid of things from older periods and using that cash to pay for new and different things. This can also be a time to reassess the whole financial picture and plan for different cash needs.

There have never been more options or information on ways to generate an income while staying home. Two websites in particular have great information on how to make some extra money while staying home with a baby. The first website is *The Dollar Stretcher* at **www.Stretcher.com**. This site has page after page devoted to ways to make staying home a viable option by saving money or generating money. In addition, the website **www.bizymoms.com** has many different ideas for stay-at-home business opportunities. It, also, has a must read page on detecting scams in work from home business opportunities.

Finally, anyone contemplating raising cash to help take care of a new family member should have a look at *Mompreneurs*, by Ellen H. Parlapiano and Patricia Cobe. They have written a book devoted to generating money as a parent. They also have a website that is well worth a look at:

www.mompreneursonline.com

Though these guides tend to be written with women in mind, there are certainly numerous opportunities for stay-at-home dads as well.

* * * * *

Part I explored common reasons why people find they suddenly need to raise cash. The process of raising cash is a goal driven process. Goals require plans, thought, and actions. Thinking and talking through options are critical steps. Planning can greatly shorten the amount of time and effort it takes to bring about the desired results. However, in the end, only action can bring results. Now that you have some idea of the specifics that apply to your situation, let's explain how to do it...

Part Two
Evaluating Your Need

Cash Flow and Budgeting

2

When people are asked if they had an emergency that had to be solved in ten minutes, how much time should be spent on planning, most say they would spend one minute on planning and nine minutes on action. When the same question was posed to astronauts, they said they would spend nine minutes on planning and one minute on doing.

This observation has some valuable wisdom for raising cash as well. Planning can be very valuable because, as the old adage goes, if you don't have the time to do it right, when will you find the time to do it over? The first step to successfully raising quick cash is to know your outcome and plan strategically.

This chapter has some specific exercises that will help you to develop the plan, you need to respond to the challenges you are facing. To have a plan, you have to have a figure in mind that will solve your temporary cash need. After you have the figure, then you need a deadline. Setting a goal for a sum of cash uses the same elements that you've used successfully in other areas of life. In addition, good plans have an order and logic to them.

This planning process should also help you evaluate alternative ways you could generate cash. There are different considerations of cost and time involved if you need to raise $50 until payday, as opposed to $10,000 for something else. Time spent on getting a true picture of how much cash you need, when you need it, and what your best available options are, will be time well spent in savings and effort. If you need $5,000 dollars in three months, that plan will require different resources and actions then will raising $50 dollars by the end of the week.

To develop the picture of what you need, you must start by examining your *cash flow*.

THE IMPORTANCE OF CASH FLOW

Cash flow analysis involves matching income against outgo. Cash is to a business, what blood is to a person. This also applies to the little businesses called lives that we all run. Unless you are a monk and you have taken a vow of poverty, a certain amount of money comes in and a certain amount of money goes out. That is called cash flow.

More than any other factor, cash flow will determine how often and how much cash you need. The single best way to get a handle on it is to get your checkbook and then raid an old board game for play money. Pay yourself your normal, expected income and then start paying bills with the play money. If at the end of the game you have money left after paying all your bills, you have *positive cash flow*. If you have run out of money, but still have bills to pay, you have *negative cash flow*. That means you are spending more than you are taking in.

Cash Flow Analysis

Sometimes the need for quick cash can be solved in other ways than raising cash. The outcome that you need right now is more money, the means to get it could be to get more cash flowing in, or it might be to stop cash from flowing out.

The most essential part of any plan is the documentation and follow through. So, when you're ready to begin the planning process, you have got to be able to write down the answers. Writing down the outcome of what you want to happen is particularly important with cash because it gives you a place to hang your *action steps* so that you can really get some traction in achieving what you want.

You have to be able to define your target of how much additional cash you're going after. Then you have to ask yourself how you plan to get there. Finally, you have to be able to create an after-quick-cash scenario that you can live with.

GOAL SETTING

Setting a goal involves asking questions about what is possible and what is desirable. Before making any decisions about raising cash, ask these questions to guide yourself through the planning process.

- ◆ Where am I now in terms of how much cash I need?
- ◆ When do I need it?
- ◆ What would I be willing to do to raise it?
- ◆ Who could I ask for it as a gift?
- ◆ Who could I borrow it from?
- ◆ What objects do I have that I could pawn to raise it?
- ◆ What could I cash in to raise the cash I need?
- ◆ What could I sell to raise the cash I need?
- ◆ What service or product could I sell to earn it?
- ◆ What sources of unclaimed cash could I have overlooked?
- ◆ What would I absolutely not be willing to do to raise it?
- ◆ How much time do I have to raise this cash?
- ◆ How much work do I want to put into raising it?
- ◆ How likely is it that a bank, credit union, or finance company will lend to me?
- ◆ How certain am I that I can repay a loan within the time frame I need?
- ◆ What would I sell in a heartbeat if I could to raise the cash?
- ◆ What would I never sell to raise it?
- ◆ What job would I do immediately if I could make money?
- ◆ What task would I never do to raise this cash, no matter how much I needed it?
- ◆ What is my back-up plan if I cannot raise the cash I need?

EVALUATING THE PLAN

A good plan takes into account the resources available to achieve the desired outcome. The chart on the next page is designed for one person who can decide by himself or herself to pursue any given strategy. If you're doing this with a partner or a spouse, each one of you may want to do a separate exercise and then compare notes. Items that are enormously valuable to one party, may be prime garage sale pickings for another. It pays to know before the items are sold.

The chart can help weigh the advantages and disadvantages of a given strategy before you carry it out.

EXAMPLE: If you only have an hour to spend on carrying out your plan to raise cash by selling off your books, but you have three months before you need the money, listing your books on **www.half.com** might be a great idea (see Chapter 5). If you need the money from selling the books in a day, then you're only alternative might be to take the books to second hand stores to sell.

The chart on the following page is for simple decision making based on *cost-benefit principles*. It is broken down as follows. The strategy you want to evaluate goes on the left hand column underneath the *Quick Cash* strategy heading. The factors you should evaluate are in the center. The third column, *value,* is for ranking each of the factors in column two. The table on the following page provides some examples you can use to develop your own ranking values.

Quick Cash Strategy	Factors	Value
	Time	
	Wait for payoff	
	Energy	
	Cost	
	Payoff	
	Need for help	
	Misery factor	
Total		

For each factor, assign a value using the following ranking:

Time	Hours	3	Days	2	Weeks	1
Wait for payoff	Hours	3	Days	2	Weeks	1
Energy	Easy	3	Moderate	2	Hard	1
Cost	Free	3	Under $10	2	Over $10	1
Payoff	Over $100	3	Over $10	2	Over $1	1
Need for help	Do It Yourself	3	Some Help	2	Professional Assistance	1
Misery factor	None	3	Bearable	2	Painful	1

Here are two examples using the chart.

Quick Cash Strategy	Factors	Value
Starting pop can	**Time**	3
recycling bag	**Wait for payoff**	1
	Energy	3
	Cost	3
	Payoff	1
	Need for help	3
	Misery factor	3
Total		*17*

Quick Cash Strategy	Factors	Value
Donate plasma	**Time**	2
	Wait for payoff	3
	Energy	1
	Cost	3
	Payoff	3
	Need for help	2
	Misery factor	1
Total		*13*

Starting to recycle pop cans will not pay very much very soon, but it is super easy and you can do it yourself. Donating your plasma, on the other hand, is something most people would have to think about it. It is painful, requires professional help, and can be inconvenient. But, it has potential (according to some estimates to raise hundreds of dollars a month), so it might be an option.

Each factor gets a number, but weighing the factors is definitely an individual experience. If you have a fear of needles and giving blood is a horrible experience, selling plasma will look like a bad deal no matter how much money it could raise. If it is one of your *what would you never do to make money*—then donating plasma is not going to be an option.

Recycling pop cans may work for most people if they have enough time or lots and lots of cans they can get quickly. The time factor is very much a personal question as well. If you are raising cash for a goal with a longer horizon, then saving pop cans or going on a major expedition to find them may be a very valuable strategy. If, on the other hand, you hate the whole idea of having to wash them out, mash them down, and haul them to the recycling plant, then it will be a bad idea—no matter how far off your goals is. (This exercise also works well for closely matched opportunities that you cannot seem to make your mind up about.)

Another set of considerations to add to your decision making process is the four Es—Effort, Energy, Expectation, and Emotion. Let's look at an example. You own your great Aunt Mildred's wildebeest with a clock in its stomach. You are thinking about selling it for some quick cash. The first factor to consider is *effort*. If it will only take five minutes to put it on eBay, that is a huge advantage, so write it down. On the other hand, if there is only one appraiser in the whole world who specializes in wildebeest clocks and she is in Borneo for six months, that is a huge disadvantage.

Second, what is the *energy* factor involved? If you have to drag the fifty pound clock to every antique store in New York City, that is a huge disadvantage and should be noted. On the other hand, if you can call up one dealer and sell it, that is pretty easy.

Third, put in the disadvantages and advantages of it in terms of how far it goes toward meeting your *expectations* and satisfying your need for quick cash. For example, if there are only five clocks like yours in the world and you need $400 and they usually sell for $20,000 at auction that is a huge advantage. On the other hand, if the clocks sell for between $30 and $40 at auction and you need to raise $5,000 for a major roof repair, it may not be worth your time.

The last factor is a purely subjective one that is actually the most important. If you adored your great-aunt Mildred and loved nothing better than hearing the story of how she acquired the wildebeest clock, then you may regret selling the clock forever. Your *emotional* attachment to the item and what it represents can override your immediate need. On the other hand, it may be cathartic to clean out old skeletons, so to speak, and make a new start.

BASIC BUDGET ANALYSIS

This is a book on raising cash fast, and yet when Ben Franklin said, "A penny saved is a penny earned," he had a point. If this were a book on how to find rhinos in the Savannah instead of how to raise cash, a lot of pages would be devoted to tracking them. There would be exhaustive sections on how to recognize their tracks and where they were likely to be found. Hunting quick cash poses many of the same challenges.

Track Spending

If you want to find cash, it definitely helps to be able to track it. One of the fastest and most effective ways to track cash is to sit down and have a heart to heart talk with your check register. Just by flipping through your check register and identifying where the money is going will put you in a spot with more control and options.

You do not have to balance it, just look at the register or your canceled checks to see what the largest expenses are for each month. After a couple of months, you will begin to see patterns. Once you see the patterns, you can make a list of the big-ticket items and see if there are ways you can knock them down. After you've nailed the big ones, start looking for smaller ones. If you can eliminate ten $50 dollar expenses or fifty $10 dollar ones at the end of the month you've saved yourself $500 dollars. Any money you can save may be a lot easier and less stressful than trying to raise the cash quickly. Cutting expenses may free up cash in a hurry that may eliminate or lessen the need for other strategies in the rest of the book.

Creditors

In general it pays to pay the *secured creditors* first. Secured creditors are the ones who have an interest in collateral you own for the loan. In the case of most people, this means the house and the car. Other creditors like credit cards and utilities are *unsecured creditors.* It may be possible to delay payments to them without suffering as much. However this strategy comes with a risk because even one missed payment on one credit card can cause a ripple effect on your credit score. So first negotiate with your creditors and try to reach an agreement that delays your payment without the consequences.

Break-Even Analysis

A *break-even analysis* is just like a financial see saw. It strives to answer at what point are expenses and income balanced. This will give you a good idea of how the money coming in and out might be arranged to lessen the need for quick cash.

The other thing that could be the solution to the problem is to think in terms of the benefit sought from raising the cash. It is sometimes helpful to determine the ultimate outcome is to see if there are different strategies that can accomplish the same end result.

EXAMPLE: Jim is looking to raise $500 to get his car fixed so he can have reliable transportation to get out and about. The end result is not necessarily $500. $500 to pay the mechanic for the parts is only a means, the end result is a reliable car. So Jim needs to also think of different strategies that can accomplish that result.

First, can he find a mechanic he can trade expertise for? This generally is most effective in small shops rather than chain stores where the owner may not have any negotiation power. But the first question is what could Jim trade for the car repair. For example, if Jim were an accountant he could do the books. If he were a lawyer he could do a will. If Jim had a clean up service, he could trade some free cleaning for the repair. If Jim has freelance writing skills he could trade a brochure for the repair.

Look at what you do have and can offer. (One of the best books around for ways to think creatively about problem solving is *A Technique for Producing Ideas* by James Webb.)

Redirect Expenses

The following A–Z list of issues identifies some ways that you can raise the cash you need by *redirecting* expenses. This redirection may provide the break-even amount needed without ever actually having to raise *new* cash.

◆ *Add-ons* like extended warranties on new purchases should be scrutinized careful.

◆ *Bank fees* can cost lots of money—never use an ATM you do not belong to.

◆ *Coupons* can be a thrifty shoppers best friend.

◆ *Do I need this or Do I want it?* This phrase alone can save you big dollars when you're raising quick cash. Any unnecessary expenses should be eliminated or delayed for as long as possible.

◆ *Eliminate the extras* such as eating out.

◆ *Frugal people check receipts* and eliminate any unnecessary expenses that have crept on to credit card bills like travel clubs.

◆ *Generics* can save you a bundle.

◆ *Heating bills payment plans* are definitely an option if you are trying to raise cash. (Turning your thermostat down one or two degrees you can save 1–2% on your heating bill.

◆ *Insurance*—It's time to go through the insurance bills with a fine tooth comb to be sure your medical insurance has paid all the claims it should. It may be time to scale back auto coverage on older cars so that you are covered in case you harm someone else in an accident, but full coverage for replacement doesn't make sense on older cars.

◆ *Just do it yourself* instead of paying for it. Any service you can do yourself that you're currently paying someone else to do is a source of immediate cash. (This can vary from cutting your children's hair to cleaning the gutters out yourself.)

◆ *Kill the cable.*

◆ *Late fees* can be money in your pocket if you can eliminate them.

◆ *Mortgages insurance* (PMI) is a major mortgage expense. If you have it, see if you can drop it.

◆ *Negotiate, Negotiate, Negotiate*—Not everything in life can be negotiated, but many things can be.

◆ *Organize* your bills and money; you can definitely increase your available cash.

◆ *Papers* and magazine subscriptions are another source of cash you can raise by cancelling them.

◆ *Quit smoking!*

◆ *Rent,* don't buy the occasional item. If you have a major tool or purchase you need, but think you'll only use it once, don't buy it—rent it.

- ◆ *Save* your pennies, dimes, and nickels too. Throw your change in a container and let it sit.
- ◆ *Thrift stores* can be a great place to bargain shop.
- ◆ *Used items* may be the better bet. A new car can depreciate almost a third of its value in the first day off of the lot. (Maybe a used car will do.)
- ◆ *Vary your diet* by eliminating or reducing meat since it is often one of the largest, if not the biggest, grocery expense.
- ◆ *Wash* instead of dry-cleaning, if it can be done safely.
- ◆ *X-out* unneeded expenses.
- ◆ *Year-end closeout sales* can also save money.
- ◆ *Zoos*, museums, and other cultural attractions have free days.

Part Three
Raising
Quick Cash

Ask For It

3

Among the oldest and most successful ways to raise cash is to ask your family and friends for it. To paraphrase the Robert Frost poem, "home is the place where you go and they have to take you in." Family and friends are the people that you go to for money, who are the most likely to feel compelled to give it to you.

Asking for cash from family and friends means basically asking for a gift. It is different from how the book uses the term *finding* (meaning finding either your own cash or finding lost valuables that have no owner that you can then turn into cash). Legal implications involved in gifts generally turn on whether the exchange was indeed really a gift. What makes a *gift* to you is a question for the specific laws of your state. However, there are some general rules.

A gift must be made voluntarily. The person giving the gift must also have the capacity to make the gift. In the legal sense *capacity* means they know what they are doing and what the results of what they are doing will be. Further, the person making the gift to you must actually complete the process of making the gift. They cannot say next year on the 23rd of April they will give you their superhero memorabilia collection. Instead, they need to put the comic books into your possession. Finally, they have to know you have received it.

On the other hand, if the transaction is not documented, it can still cause problems. If there are siblings involved and one is always borrowing money and the others are not, then that may strain family relationships. You can the money problems easier than you can solve the family fights that may come out of them. It is wise to be cautious when borrowing money from family and friends.

In addition to flesh and blood relatives, everybody also has an Uncle Sam in the form of the U.S. Government. Your Uncle Sam may be a place to look for a source of cash or benefits that may free up other cash. Asking for money from the government or appropriate charity still can have enormous social stigmas attached to it. But, at the same time, federal and state programs exist to be used. They can be a great source of resources when all other resources have been exhausted.

One very important thing to keep in mind about using government programs is that they are meant to be temporary. Government programs are designed to be a safety net during a precarious time. After the times get better, peoples' lives improve and they stop needing and using the government programs.

Now is not the time to be too proud to use the tools that come to hand. If you need cash or the things that cash can buy and you need them in a hurry, get moving and get into action to tap all the resources that are available.

FAMILY AND FRIENDS

Asking family and friends for cash may not be the easiest or most pleasant thing to do. Asking may require a significant loss in pride or it may require revisiting old family issues. In addition, there are some serious drawbacks to asking family and friends for money. First, it may all be for naught. Just as your loved ones might love to help you, they also may not have the means. Those who are most sympathetic and willing to help, may well be those who most desperately need what money they have for their own purposes. Your aged relatives, who are on social security and a pension, may themselves be better prospects to give money to, than to receive money from.

If you decide to ask family and friends for money, you need to give the possibility of rejection some serious thought. If you ask for help and your closest friends, family, and allies fail to give it to you, it is hard not to take it personally. And yet, it may not be personal. Often times the financial struggles of those closest to us are mysteries. Also, the people may love you, but loath what you will do with the money.

When you need cash and need it quickly, it's easy to get tunnel vision and think of things only in terms of money. It is hard not to want to hunker down. But unless you live in a vault, you are not likely to find a lot of cash at home that you have not already found. This is the time to get out and about and to think the most creatively you possibly can.

Family and friends may not give you money, but they may serve as a source for raising cash another way.

The chart below is designed to tap into your friends and family as resources that can help you find your way through the current cash crunch. People who would have no hesitation calling their friends and family for help finding a pediatrician or a plumber often sit paralyzed in front of the phone when they need to tap into their network for help with a financial problem.

This chart is designed to break the ice; shatter the inhibitions; and, get you smiling and dialing on the road to actions. Raising cash is a process of actions, sometimes constant and unrelenting action, but it all starts with the first call. This exercise is designed to help you focus your resources so they have some leverage behind them.

Start by making a chart with the following headings.

Who are they	How do I know them	Best quality	Like to listen to	Hate to listen to	Who do they know	So what

These headings are designed to answer the following questions.

◆ Who are they?

◆ How do I know them?

◆ If I had to sell my best friend on a blind date what would I say this person's best quality was?

◆ What do they talk about that I like to listen to?

◆ What do they drone on endlessly about that bores me?

◆ Who do they know?

◆ Can it lead to raising cash?

By answering these questions, you will be able to pull out the information you need to see *if* and *how* they can help solve your cash flow problem.

Let's look at an example using your Aunt Mildred. Before you considered this, she was just your aunt. Now let's walk through this in terms of what she might need that you can offer relieving a need for both of you. Fill in the chart by answering the questions about what you know about Aunt Mildred.

Who are they	How do I know them	Best quality	Like to listen to	Hate to listen to	Who do they know	So what
Aunt Mildred	Family	Nice	Family Stories	Cat Problems Collector Stories	Other Retired People	

Aunt Mildred is retired and she has cats. The cats are driving her crazy because she has to take them to the vet, as do all of her other retired friends who have pets. Before you needed cash, this was just another dreaded topic of conversation at Thanksgiving. Now it's an opportunity. You can take the cat to the vet for her. In fact, you could chauffeur all of her cats and all of her friends cats to the vets for a modest fee.

It doesn't end there. One of the other topics she talks about that drives you crazy is her collecting tendency. Let's say she collects depression glass. It's a common collectible and many people do. If you have any of it and need to raise cash, she is now a resource you could not pay enough money to have. She knows what it's worth; where it's sold; and, who to sell it to. Why go on eBay when you have her? In fact, she can probably help you put it on eBay and might be delighted to do so for you.

When you've got a financial crisis and you need to raise cash, it may be the time in your life when you least want to worry about other people and their problems. However, this is also a time when it can pay to develop your relationships and consider others' physical health.

GOVERNMENTAL PROGRAMS

People get indirect money benefits from the federal government all the time without any criticism or embarrassment. Individuals take out FHA loans or student loans that are underwritten by the federal government all the time. Unemployment benefits as well as those available upon the death of a spouse are also routinely taken.

Other programs also exist that should be taken advantage of if you qualify and have a need. For example, some townships offer general assistance to people who live in their borders but do not qualify for other forms of government assistance. These programs can sometimes be found on the web or they can be researched by calling the local township office.

Townships may also operate food pantries for the benefit of their residents. Signing up for unemployment compensation doesn't have a lot of social stigma attached to it, but signing up for the food pantry might. The crucial thing to remember about government programs is that they are supposed to be temporary, and they usually are. These programs are umbrellas, not roofs. Once the downpour passes, most people transition off of them quickly.

Unemployment Compensation

Unemployment compensation can literally be a lifesaver for the person suffering from a job loss. It is a program made up of federal and state laws that was put into place during the Great Depression in the 30's. Its two overriding objectives are to help workers who have become unemployed through no fault of their own and to smooth out the effect of the U.S. business cycle.

The major questions anyone interested in unemployment compensation wants to know are: *Do I qualify* and *How do I apply*? First, if your job loss is part of a plant closing, then representatives from the state office of unemployment compensation may come to your job site. They will cover the basics of how to apply for unemployment benefits, contact information, and where to go. If, however, the job loss is not part of a plant closing, you'll need to contact the state office yourself.

State unemployment offices are listed in the section of the phone book that lists government agencies. You will need to call them or go online to find their website to get the particulars. Procedures will vary from state to state. Some states will require applicants to physically go to the local unemployment office. In some, you may be able to complete the whole process by phone or mail.

As soon as you lose your job, you should file for unemployment. It takes time to get the paper work rolling through the system. As a general rule, you should figure a couple of weeks before you get the first check. To get the benefits and to keep getting the benefits, there are requirements that you must be aware of. First, you have to be able to supply the address of your old job, how long you worked there, plus, wage and salary information. In order to keep getting unemployment benefits, there are other requirements that may vary from state to state about looking for work and reporting income from work, as well as registering with the employment offices of the state for possible job openings.

The state agency makes the actual decision whether or not you qualify for *unemployment*. States also make determinations about how long individuals can draw unemployment. All states have specific and different requirements, but there are some common elements. First, you have to have been unemployed during some set period. Usually it is a certain number of quarters. Second, you have to be unemployed (no new job) and it cannot be your fault that you are unemployed. For example, if you quit, it may be hard to qualify for unemployment. However, if the employer makes the decision to close the office where you are working, then the loss of the job is not your fault. Also, keep in mind that even if your employer fires you, you may still be able to qualify for unemployment benefits if you can establish that your employer was wrong or unfair in his or her decision to terminate you.

The amount you will be eligible for in benefits is determined by your salary or wages over the last year. However, states generally impose caps on unemployment benefits by limiting the size of the benefit and by limiting the eligible period. Unless there are periods of bad national unemployment, the benefits will only last for twenty-six weeks—at the most. If the economy is bad or your state has suffered exceptional job losses, then there *may* be extensions of unemployment benefits available. In addition, during times of very bad unemployment, your state may make grants for retraining available.

Like all government programs, only the government can actually tell you whether you qualify for unemployment benefits, or for an extension of benefits, and how much your benefit will be. The individual state office that administers unemployment benefits for the part of the state where your former employer was located should be able to tell you for sure whether you qualify.

If, for whatever reason, they deny your claim, ask about how to appeal. As a general rule, programs administered by the state and or federal government, have avenues through which you can appeal a denial of a claim for benefits. (For unemployment purposes, the District of Columbia counts as a state.)

Social Security Benefits

Social security benefits are a source of cash. There is a *lump sum death benefit* of $255 that is available to the surviving spouse of a covered worker. Social security can be reached at 800-772-1213 or at **www.ssa.gov**. Have the following documents available to file your claim:

◆ the survivor's and/or decedent's social security number;
◆ the certified death certificate;
◆ your marriage certificate;
◆ your birth certificate;
◆ divorce papers from previous marriages, if applicable;
◆ the deceased's W-2 forms or tax returns; and,
◆ the bank account you want the money to be deposited into.

In addition to the lump sum benefit, survivors may also be able to receive other benefits. For example, *survivor's benefits* are available if the claimant is over 60 years of age, is a spouse, or is at least 50 years of age and disabled. In addition, children may also be able to claim survivors benefits, providing they are under 18 years of age (19 years of age if they are full-time students), not married, or disabled under certain circumstances.

Veterans Benefits

If your spouse was a veteran, you may qualify for additional benefits. Many people are familiar with the *funeral benefits* that families of veterans receive. However you may qualify for some monetary benefits as well. You can contact the Department of Veteran Affairs at 800-827-1000 or at **www.va.gov**. They can tell you what benefits you may qualify for.

One particular benefit that may be helpful is the *death pension*. This is a payment by the government to you to raise your income to the level of the pension. The pension is designed to help out the surviving spouse of veterans who meet certain service requirements. This benefit is currently paying out about $981 a month in benefits.

There is another benefit that pays out monetary benefits to surviving spouses and children of veterans who fit certain service requirements as well. There are several ways a veteran's survivor may qualify for this program, and only the Department of Veteran Affairs can say for sure whether or not a surviving spouse or child qualifies. Generally, the program applies to veterans who have either been killed in active duty or who have suffered injuries in active duty that later led to their deaths.

Food Stamps

The *food stamp* program is a federal program. The U.S. Department of Agriculture administers it. States then administer it locally and may have slightly different eligibility requirements than what the federal government does.

It is essentially a *means-driven* program. If what you earn or otherwise receive in income and what you own fit within certain guidelines, you will be eligible. If not, then you won't be.

There are web resources that can be very helpful in guiding you through this process. The federal website is at:

www.foodstamps-step1.usda.gov

This also has a step-by-step guide to applying for food stamps.

Application

The first thing you need is the application. You can apply at the local food stamp office in person using their application form. You can also call and request a form and have it mailed to you or you can often get the form at your state's website. There also may be other places you can find the forms. The website instructs applicants that they should do the first part at the food stamp office and leave it there for immediate processing. Then you have to do an interview with the stamp office. You need documents establishing identity and financial need. For instance, if you are paying child support you should bring canceled checks.

Eligibility

If you are denied, you have a right to appeal. The phone numbers for food stamp offices are listed in the government sections of the phone books. The federal government has a toll free number at 800-221-5689. As a rule of thumb, figure that if you have more than $2,000 in assets you probably will not be eligible. However, there is a list of things that you should not count, such as your house, 401(k), and burial plots.

State eligibility may vary, so if you think you're possibly eligible, check with the state office to see. For example, some states count your car in to the asset mix and some do not. Also, if you receive supplemental security income benefits or state cash assistance programs, you will be able to have those not counted in. There may be other exceptions that apply in your state.

If you do qualify, you get an *electronic benefits transfer* (EBT) card that allows stores to debit your food stamp account directly. Food stamps can only be used for food and seeds to grow food. There are many things it cannot be used for like alcohol, tobacco, and hot food among others. If you have question you should go to the website or call the local office.

Emergency Situations

If you have an emergency food situation, you should file the paper-work in person and ask if there are procedures in place to help people who have an emergency need for food stamps and other benefits. Some states allow emergency benefits such as pre-investigative cash assistance or expedited food stamps. In some situations your application may be processed in a week. You will be eligible for expedited food stamps if you meet certain income requirements. However, if you want to keep on receiving food stamps, you need to complete the regular application process.

WIC

The *Special Supplemental Nutrition Program for Women, Infants and Children* (WIC) is a federal program for woman and children that is designed to provide low-income participants with nutritional food. The United States Department of Agriculture (USDA) oversees the WIC program.

Like food stamps, eligibility depends on how much the family owns and how much they owe. Your income must be at or below the poverty guidelines. Basically, if you qualify for food stamps, Medicaid, or temporary assistance, you will probably qualify for WIC. The federal government estimates that almost half of all the babies in the U.S. receive WIC benefits. WIC has a priority system in place to make sure pregnant woman and children get first access to benefits. The website for the USDA is located at **www.fns.usda.gov**.

HOT LUNCH PROGRAM

In addition to these programs, the food and nutrition service of the USDA also administers the national *hot lunch program* for school children. These programs are designed to allow low-income children to get nutritious food, while allowing the USDA to help provide marketing opportunities for American agriculture.

The USDA gives schools cash and free agricultural commodities that the school uses to run its lunch and after school snack program. The program is based on income eligibility guidelines supplied by the USDA. Generally household income must be no more than 130% of the national poverty level, and household assets must not be greater than $2,000. The school itself determines eligibility. A small percentage of applicants are randomly selected for income verification. If you are receiving food stamps or Temporary Aid to Needy Families (TANF) already you will be eligible.

TEMPORARY AID TO NEEDY FAMILIES

When welfare reform was passed, *Temporary Aid to Needy Families* (TANF) was what replaced it. It is a means-based program available for families and individuals who fit within certain income and means guidelines. Although it is a federal program, states administer it and set their own rules on who is eligible.

TANF is a work-based program with time limits on receiving assistance. Generally, a person is limited to no more than five years of benefits. Within two years of receiving benefits, the recipient must be engaged in a work activity. That means he or she must be working or receiving training.

The application process is run by the individual states. State departments will be listed in the yellow pages or online. Usually these programs are called *family services* or *children services*. The states also impose different requirements for owning property. Some states require that people only have $1,000 worth of property to qualify. There are also procedures to appeal if you feel you should have received benefits and were wrongfully denied.

EARNED INCOME CREDIT

If you qualify, you may get money back from the federal government on your taxes. There is a tax break known as the *earned income credit*. This is a tax credit *(refund)* that individuals and families may qualify for if they fit within certain low to medium income levels. It does not directly give you cash, but it lowers your federal income taxes so you may qualify for a refund. You still need to have worked and you still must have paid income taxes. You can get more information on the IRS website at **www.irs.gov**. Libraries and post offices may also have the IRS pamphlet that explains it.

Qualifications

To get a rough idea of whether you qualify, your income for 2003 must be less than $29,666 for a taxpayer with one qualifying child or $30,666 for married taxpayers filing jointly. If you have more than one qualifying child, you can have income up to $33,692. If you have more than one child, are married and filing jointly, you can have income up to $34,692. If you have no children and are not married or are filing by yourself you can earn up to $11,230. It would be $12,230 for married filing jointly.

The IRS publication is number 596. There is a form in it where you can quickly add up your income to see if you can qualify. This publication is available at the IRS website at **www.irs.gov**. Another good source of information on the earned income credit can be found at **www.taxcreditresources.org**. This site has good information about other websites. It also has a simple eligibility program that can let you know if you qualify and how much you might expect.

If you are going to file a claim with the IRS to get the earned income credit, you should investigate to see if you could qualify for the *advance payment option*. This would allow you to have an extra $50 added to your pay on a biweekly basis. You may not be able to get the whole amount of the credit this way, but you could get some and the rest would be yours when you filed your annual tax return. You will need to submit a form *W-5* to the IRS.

You can usually get this credit without it disqualifying you for other government benefits such as social security supplementary income, food stamps, Section 8 low income housing, and Medicaid.

If the thought of figuring taxes on your own fills you with dread, you can use the *volunteer income tax assistance program* (VITA). You can find a local office by calling the IRS at 800-829-1040.

State Programs
In addition to the federal program, several states and the District of Columbia also have programs as well. The states that have a program are Illinois, Indiana, Iowa, Kansas, Maine, Maryland, Massachusetts, Minnesota, New Jersey, New York, Oklahoma, Oregon, Rhode Island, Vermont, and Wisconsin. The state revenue service should be able to tell you if your state has an earned income credit for sure.

CHARITIES
One of the main ideas in this book is to ask the crucial question, "How will I come up with cash quickly?" Additionally, people also

need to ask, "What will the cash be used for once it is found or raised?" Food is a basic and fundamental concern. Money that does not have to be spent on food is money that can be used for other things. Many communities and other not-for-profit organizations operate food pantries and food banks. These can be potent resources during tough times. Of course, like other government programs, there are issues. First of all, many government and community need-based programs carry a stigma, these are no exception. But if one of these programs will help you hang on until things improve, be the first one in line for help.

FOOD BANKS

There are local resources that can assist you. Food banks and pantries are community-based organizations that distribute to individuals who qualify. Food banks and pantries have their own individual application processes. It is usually a means-based process like many other benefits geared toward low-income individuals and families. This means filling out an application and disclosing all the financial resources that are available. It also means proving that you live in the geographic area that the food pantry serves.

In addition, food banks may impose restrictions on how much food they give away and how often people can come to use their services. For instance, some may allow only one trip per month and may only allow a certain number of days of food.

One of the major groups involved in food banks is *America's Second Harvest*. Their website can be found at **www.secondharvest.org**. They have a food bank locator feature on their website that allows people to find food banks by state, city, and zip code.

TRAVELERS AID

Traveling can be a frightening experience in itself, but to lose all your money while traveling is truly terrifying. If you lose all your cash while traveling, one of the few places that will help you raise cash right away, may be the local pawnshop. This assumes, of course, that you have something of value to pawn. If you truly have nothing, then the people to call are the *Travelers Aid Society*.

Many urban areas and airports have chapters of the Travelers Aid Society. These groups often have professional counselors who can quickly help the distressed traveler with basic needs. This groups has been helping people for a long time. Travelers Aid is a charity that was founded during the American rush westward in the 1800s. Before there were any other support systems besides family and friends, many pioneers, and especially children, wound up in strange cities with nobody to care for them.

Today, Travelers Aid is a national association of local groups that help distressed travelers. These local groups and organizations will probably not give you cash, but they can help you with temporary shelter and food needs until you can raise cash other ways. Find them online at **www.travelersaid.org** or in the Yellow Pages. In addition, they have facilities in several major airports in the U.S.

Borrow It

4

Shakespeare may have had a point when he wrote "neither a lender nor a borrower be." His observation, however, does not fit with many contemporary Americans who live off borrowed funds. Borrowing money may, in fact, be the most popular and prevalent strategy used for raising cash.

Borrowing money and pawning objects for money are very similar, yet different. At its most basic level, a *loan* is nothing more than a promise to pay a certain amount of money, plus an agreed amount of interest at a date in the future. In a loan arrangement, the loan may be secured or unsecured. *Secured loans* have some sort of *collateral* behind them that helps to ensure that the borrower will get paid back. *Unsecured loans* do not have any collateral and are only a promise to pay.

Pawning is a secured loan. When people pawn things they give an item of value to the pawnbroker who holds the item as security for their loan. If they don't pay, the pawnbroker takes their item and sells it to recover the cost of the loan.

Borrowing money is a stressful experience. It means offering up something of value in return for a loan. The *something of value* can be collateral, such as your house or car, or simply your good name in return for the loan of the money. This can be a very valuable strategy for dealing with cash crunches, but it can also be a roller coaster.

Consumer lending is a highly regulated activity. The federal government and individual states have long recognized the inequalities of position between borrowers and lenders. Many different laws have been passed to regulate the process and to protect consumers when they borrow money. The one law that consumers should be most aware of is the *Truth in Lending Act* or *Consumer Credit Protection Act*. The Truth in Lending law basically requires that lenders accurately disclose all the terms of the loan. There are two great resources for understanding laws that protect consumers. One is the Federal Trade Commission website at **www.ftc.gov**. The other is the Federal Reserve website at **www.federalreserve.gov/pubs/consumerhdbk**, which has a consumer guide to credit laws that is very helpful.

Borrowing money is not something limited to just banks and credit unions though. Many of the places that may be the consumer's best source for borrowed money may be mortgage companies or consumer finance companies. In addition, consumers may borrow against life insurance and 401(k) plans.

FAMILY AND FRIENDS

Nobody on the planet is too old for a quick loan from a family member. Although these are the trickiest of loans and it pays to think long and hard before you borrow money from family and friends, they are definitely an option to consider. When nobody else will help you, often your family and friends will.

Think long and hard about how you will repay these type of loans. Regular creditors under the *Fair Debt Collection Act* are required to follow many different procedures and rules about how they can contact you regarding past due loans. The *Fair Debt Collection Act* applies to the conduct of bill collectors and regulates when they can call and also spells out defenses and rights of consumers. Nothing limits Aunt Thelma from mentioning the loan every time you see her. You should know going in whether or not you want this type of pressure going in. You may decide a cash advance from a credit card at a high interest rate is a much better deal than the grief and embarrassment.

If you decide to go through with a loan from family or friends there are things to consider. To be successful, these loans should be written down and documented. They should allow the lender to receive a reasonable return on their money. This may introduce an element of arms length dealing into a friendship or family relationship that is just too uncomfortable for you.

An agreement over an unsecured personal loan can be written up as a *promissory note*. Promissory notes are available online and where office forms are sold. They are pretty basic forms that spell out how much the loan is for, when it's due, and what the interest rate is. Never borrow money from family members you aren't sure you can repay. Even more so than in commercial loans, the downside of not being able to pay the loan back needs to be considered since there is usually more than just money riding on the line with these kind of loans.

Although these loans do have the perils, they also have several plus factors. Family loans are often the source of money that makes many of the good things in life possible for many people. When the process works, it can work so well that the many successful loans between family members pass without notice. For example, so many down payments for first-time homes are loans from parents. Also, many college and graduate educations are paid for with loans directly or indirectly from grandparents.

Informal Agreements

Friends often make deals with friends to borrow money on items and repay them when they can. These are informal agreements such *as I'll let you keep my favorite fishing pole for $50. If I don't pay within six months, you can keep or sell the pole.* Of all the possible ways to do a secured transaction, this may be the easiest. All you need is a friend with money, who is willing to lend it, and some item you are willing to give to them to hold as security. The beauty of this arrangement is that it's all informal and all up to you and your friend. It can be done with a handshake and an agreement.

The major advantage to this way of doing things is that it is so very fast and easy.

The main disadvantage to this way of doing things is that it can easily wind up as a muddled mess and lost friendships. One important warning is that just because an agreement is informal does not necessarily mean that it is not a binding and legal agreement. Contracts over $500 or that deal with real estate, generally have to be in writing. However, oral contracts for less than that amount are also valid and binding. But, with nothing in writing, ownership of the property and the terms and conditions for the return of the property can become confused and forgotten.

Fraudulent Conveyances

There is a legal doctrine known as *fraudulent conveyances* that also comes into play when friends and family do business. Basically this legal doctrine protects the rights of creditors from the effects of certain friendly transactions. People who know that they may be sued to collect a debt or that they may be forced into bankruptcy have a powerful incentive to protect property they own by transferring it to their friends and family to keep it safe from creditors. If the person who owes the money, transfers the property to hinder or delay the creditor or if they transfer it for less than fair market value, then the court may invalidate the transfer.

If you are contemplating bankruptcy, then different factors come into play. If you are sued or go bankrupt, the court might closely scrutinize your financial life. This scrutiny includes looking at any loans or transfers of property that you have made to friends and relatives. If you try to get rid of assets after you are sued so that you have nothing left to pay a judgment, a court may conclude you have made a fraudulent conveyance. Courts will put aside these transfers and let the creditors attach your assets as if the transfer had not been made.

BANKS AND CREDIT UNIONS

Banks are in the business of lending money to consumers and business. They are very much for profit lending institutions. The banks loan the money to consumers in return for the repayment of the principal with interest over a set period. Banking is a highly regulated industry. Both state and federal laws apply to banking transactions. These laws require truth in lending and equal opportunity access to lending institutions.

Credit unions are quite different from banks in one very important way. Credit unions are not-for-profit institutions established to help their members. Banks are generally open to the public. If you've got the money, banks will generally take it. (Although banks routinely check credit histories, including in particular the history regarding checking accounts since customers who bounce checks can increase administrative costs for banks.)

Credit unions, on the other hand, require that members have some common affinity. This can mean that you work for the same company or live in the same geographic area. Credit union members pool their savings and then lend it to each other for cars and houses. Credit unions have great advantages over banks for individual investors in that they can have less stringent lending requirements and much lower service fees. Although credit unions use many of the same underwriting requirements for lending that banks do, your character and willingness to repay the money you borrow may make a difference with a credit union. Anymore, local banks are more likely to go by your credit score than whether or not they know who you are.

In both banks and credit unions, the actual process of lending the money is much the same. If you want to borrow money, you have to fill out an application that will ask pretty standard questions about your assets and job history as well as personal information designed to make sure they have the right person when they do the credit checks.

The Three Cs

Bankers used to say they lent on the three Cs—*Character, Cash,* and *Collateral.* In the old days of banking when it was a much more personal process, the C of character counted for a lot more than it does now. Today that C should probably be changed to read credit score.

A *credit score* is a number that is crunched out of the credit report and a series of weighted averages and factors. Basically, it serves as a rough and ready guide to how likely the person is going to pay off the loan.

Cash is pretty self-explanatory. If a person has a million dollars in cash on deposit at the bank and wants to borrow $10,000, his or her chances of getting the loan approved are very good indeed.

Collateral is what a person puts up that the bank can sell if they do not pay the loan in full. Part of the reason most people can get a home loan is that the house serves as the collateral. Don't pay off the loan—the bank sells the house.

Banks and credit unions are a so-so place to look for money if you're broke and need it in a hurry because that's not the business that most banks are in. If you think back to the three factors on which banks lend: credit scores, collateral, and cash, lending from a bank is really only easy and fast if you have all of those three working for you to some degree.

The trick with bank financing is to line it up when your financial life is in good shape. If you know you're going to be laid off and you think you'll need cash, arrange the home equity line while you've still got a job and life is good. Banks are like an umbrella company that won't sell their products when it rains. As long as your credit score is high and you have some cash flow—a job and some collateral, banks will probably lend. That leaves out many of the people who are reading this book and need cash quickly.

Banks and credit unions used to be more willing and responsive to the small lender who just needed to borrow a small amount of cash quickly. Now banks want to be certain the loan can be paid for out of existing cash flow. This leads to the *Three C* analysis working. First, the *cash flow* numbers must tell the banker that the person has enough money coming in he or she can pay off the loan.

Second, the *credit score* has to tell the banker the person is willing to pay off the loan. Banks drive down the road using the rear view mirror. If the person has generated sufficient cash in the past and paid their bills on time then the bank and credit union assumes they will in the future.

The problem with this, for people who need to raise cash quickly, is that something may have changed that affects one of the factors. Also, people, such as the self-employed, do not fit easily into banking categories so it's harder for them to borrow money. In addition, people without good credit histories are at a huge disadvantage now.

Credit histories are routinely checked for areas where they arguably have little value such as job applications and insurance. The relationship seems pretty tenuous between paying bills on time and driving safely, but nonetheless, insurance companies are beginning to rely more and more on credit scores.

The last factor of *collateral* presents a challenge for both the person in need of quick cash and the bank or credit union. A couple in need of money may rightly observe that they have a house worth a $100,000 and a car worth $3,000, but they can't get the bank to lend them a thousand dollars to remove the tree roots that are closing up their sewers. Their loan may have to come from the person doing the sewer work because he or she knows that they will have a lien on the house for the work so they may be willing to take a chance on the person paying because they are covered by the lien.

But the bank or credit union would look at that same situation and apply the three C analysis. If the person was employed and his or her credit score was ok, the bank or credit union might lend the money as an unsecured loan. That means the bank does not have any collateral it can sell if the person doesn't pay. Basically they are betting that based on the credit score (history of paying in the past) and cash flow (how much money they have made) that they will get paid without resorting to collateral. This is the business that banks and credit unions like to be in.

But, here's the rub. If the person owns their own house, has a car as noted above, but has no source of income, then the bank or credit union will be a lot less enthused about lending them money. Even if the person has a house worth a lot and a car worth a lot, the bank does not want to have to take them and sell them to recover the money that it loaned out.

Some lending institutions are, however, *collateral lenders*. The classic example of a collateral lender is a pawnshop. If that same person had a Rolodex watch worth $10,000, the bank wouldn't care if the person came in and handed it to the loan officer and said, *its worth $10,000 you can sell it in a week if I don't pay you back*. Pawnshops are discussed in greater detail beginning on page 81.

Many different factors influence a person's chances of getting a loan. As noted, the major factors with a bank, credit union, or finance company will be the credit score, cash flow, and collateral put up for the loan.

Overdraft Protection

Traditional *overdraft protection* is designed to help bank customers avoid nonsufficient fees from accidentally bouncing checks. Basically, this is an unsecured personal *line of credit*. A line of credit is a loan for a maximum amount of money and a certain time and interest rate that renews itself as you pay it down. The fact that it's unsecured means you don't have to put up something like a house or your car to secure the loan. However, some overdraft arrangements may be tied to a home equity line of credit. You should know, going in, what kind of loan you are going to have. With unsecured personal lines of credit, banks are limited in what they can take from you to satisfy the note if you fail to pay. However, in the case of a home equity line of credit, the loan is secured ultimately by your house. The bank may foreclose if you fail to pay.

This is basically designed to be a short-term loan you can get by simply asking for the money after you have set it up. For example, if you only have $100 in your checking account, but write a check for $120, the bank will advance money in preset amounts to recover the check. In this case, the bank would put an extra $100 in your account to cover the $20 overage.

There is a limit to the amount of money banks will loan for overdraft protection. Think in terms of $500 to $2500. There also may be a fee to apply. However, overdraft protection is a *revolving line of credit*. That means if you pay it down, the full amount becomes available for to use against.

Banks and credit unions often offer overdraft as a service to their customers. If you don't already need it, you will need to set it up by setting up an application with a bank.

The beauty of this type of loan is that it should be fairly fast to set up and use. You set it up by filling out forms and you can activate it by writing checks. This type of arrangement gives the borrower two very valuable resources. First, it truly is quick cash that is available right away without a lot of paperwork and delays. Second, it can save you a lot of money in bounced check fees and damages.

Of course there are also some disadvantages. For one thing, you have to have a checking account. Many people do not have checking accounts. Secondly, the bank has to approve you for the overdraft. Banks routinely screen customers and if they have bounced too many checks, they will not offer them an account. The other disadvantage is that if it becomes a permanent loan, the interest rates can be relatively high. However, the rate will still be cheaper than cash advances from credit cards.

Another disadvantage is that this is a loan with limits. Depending on the exact requirements of your bank, you may be required to pay off all the balance within a certain period of time. Also, these kinds of loans generally are only available in a range instead of an exact amount. For example, if you bounce a check for $138.50 you may have to borrow $200.00 to cover it.

People who want to pursue this as an option should be aware that not all overdraft protection is created equal. Banks have noted the success of the payday loan centers and some of them are now offering a similar product. Further, more and more banks are allowing overdraft protection to come from a savings account or credit card. The money comes out of whatever account the customer arranges in advance, so that part is ok, but if the money comes out of a credit card, you run the risk of racking up substantial interest fees.

Bounce Protection

Bounce protection is a different product. Banks advertise this as a product that will allow customers to overdraw their account by a set amount ranging from $500 to a $1,000 dollars. But if the customer writes checks for more than the set amount, the bank may not cover the checks. The bank will not waive the nonsufficient fund fee so the customer will pay the fee, which is usually somewhere between $25 on the low end and $40 on the high end. Additionally, the customer has to pay a daily fee ranging from a couple of dollars upwards to more than $10 if the account is not brought into balance.

Think about how this math could work if you overdraw the account—you'll pay $35 plus a daily fee. On a $200 overdraft you could easily pay $40 which is equivalent to a 20% interest rate. At rates like that, you may be able to get a cash advance on your credit card for a lesser amount that you would not have to pay off within thirty days.

For more information on this option, read a research paper done by the *National Consumer Law Center* at:

www.consumerlaw.org/initiatives/test_and_comm/appendix.shtml

Refinancing

The recent run of low interest rates fueled a huge boom in *refinancing* that allowed many people to accomplish two things. They were able to take money out of their houses to use for other things and lower their interest rates on their *mortgage*. A mortgage is an agreement where a lender loans money out to a borrower in return for repayment of the money with interest and a *security interest* in the real property. Real property consists of buildings and land. A security interest means that the borrower agrees to let the lender sell the property if he or she doesn't repay the loan. This agreement is know as the security interest agreement.

In a usual mortgage, the lender loans the money to the borrower to purchase the land or building. The lender then takes a security interest that allows the lender to foreclose or take over the property and sell it off if the borrower doesn't make the payments on the loan.

FICO

Refinancing residential real estate is a very popular strategy for raising money. However, this option depends on your ability to borrow money. Your credit score is a very important factor in both whether your loan application will be approved and what interest rate you'll pay. One of the best guides to your credit score is the website of the

Fair Isaac company that developed it at **www.myfico.com**. They call it the FICO. Each of the three main credit bureaus has a different name for it. Each bureau also has subtle differences in how they calculate it.

The FICO score works out to a number between the 400s and the 800s. In this case, it's better to have a high number. Several different factors go into the credit score, but one of the most important is timeliness in paying bills. The difference in interest rates for different credit scores is quite significant. In the example the website uses, a person with a score of 500 to 599 could expect to pay 9.28 percent for a loan, while a person who had a score of 720-850 could acquire the same thirty-year fixed rate mortgage for 5.771%. Over the course of a thirty-year mortgage, this amounts a huge difference in payments.

On a $150,000 loan, the lower interest rate of 5.771% would make the monthly payment $877 and the total interest rate paid would amount to $165,850. If the person with lower credit score applied they would have a loan payment of $1,238 and a total interest payment of $295,772. A difference of over $100,000 over the course of the loan would be the result.

The first question to ask when contemplating refinancing is whether after the fees it will be worth it. The rule of thumb is that if refinancing will lower your interest rate by at least two percentage points and you plan on being in the house for three years after you refinance, then it will be worth it.

ARMs

Generally speaking, people want to either save money, reduce risk, or raise money when they refinance. If they bought the house during a high interest rate period, refinancing with a lower interest rate can reduce their mortgage payments significantly. Some mortgages are what are known as *adjustable rate mortgages* or ARMs. This means that the interest rate, and thus the payment on the loan, can go up when the interest rates go up. Many people find this risk uncomfortable and wish to lock in a stable and hopefully significantly lower rate.

Additionally, some refinancers may want to shorten their mortgage pay off periods. Finally, refinancing is one of the major ways people can tap into the equity values in their real estate to raise cash. It may pay to check with the current mortgage holder to see if they would be willing to refinance the mortgage in order to keep the loan. Getting a new mortgage to replace the old one is really much the same process as getting a mortgage in the first place. (Other options for using your home to raise cash such as *second mortgages* and *home equity loans* are discussed later in this section.)

Refinancing has all of the same costs associated with it that a mortgage does. Real estate loans require application fees, attorneys fees possibly, appraisal fees, proof of insurance tile search, and other possible fees such as mortgage insurance and a home inspection.

Prepayment Penalty

However, the biggest problem in refinancing isn't a fee, it's a penalty in the form of a *prepayment penalty*. If your current mortgage has a prepayment penalty, then you may have to abandon the idea of refinancing. Many government loans do not have prepayment penalties, but private lenders may impose them on borrowers. Basically, a prepayment penalty forces you to pay a penalty for paying off the loan early.

Of the loans that are available, *residential mortgages* are some of the most regulated and paper intensive. Like other loans, a mortgage starts with an application form. The application form is designed to produce information on two things—you and the property you want to buy. For you, the bank is interested in employment and credit info. For the property, the lending institution is interested in the how much it's worth and what kind of house it is.

Many different federal laws come into play during the lending process. For example, your credit report and score are key elements in getting a mortgage. These important items are governed by the *Fair Credit Reporting Act*. In addition, lenders may not discriminate based on certain factors including race, religion, and national origin among other factors. These protections are spelled out in the *Equal Credit Opportunity Act* as well as the *Fair Housing Act*.

Since lenders rely so heavily on credit reports and credit score, if you only do one thing to try to improve your chances for a mortgage at the rate you want, that one thing should be to read your credit report before you apply. Lenders are particularly interested in not only whether you pay bills, but also whether you pay them on time.

Under federal law, you have a clear right to access your credit file. You also have rights to request corrections of information that is not accurate. Contact information on the credit agencies can be found in Appendix B as well as online and in the Yellow Pages. If you have recently applied for credit and been denied, you have the right to receive a free copy of your credit report.

Lenders need to know how much you plan on borrowing. With conventional mortgages, this number is based on your available income and the property's estimated value. The lender will require an *appraisal.* Appraisals count for a lot because the banker wants to be sure that if you fail to pay then the house can be sold to recover the balance of the loan. The only way for the lender to be absolutely sure of the value of the house would be to sell the property, which is not very practical. The second best thing is to compare your house with a certain number, usually at least two similar ones like that, have sold recently in the same general area. The appraisal can be a magic number for you as the borrower because usually the lender will lend up to a certain stated percentage of the value. Usually this number is fairly high—think above 70% at least. However, if it is a second home or other issues come up, the lender may not be willing to lend as much.

A mortgage is not necessarily the fastest way to raise cash since you should figure on the order of thirty days. If you are seeking a FHA or VA loan, figure a longer time frame. They are also not the cheapest loans because you have the fees, the appraisal and closing costs. However, real estate, along with pension rights, are often the largest asset people have available. It is an option that should not be overlooked. Also interest rates on mortgages are among the lower ones that consumers may encounter.

Reverse Mortgages

A *reverse mortgage* allows a person who is sixty-two years old or older to use their house as security to borrow a lump sum. The lump sum is paid out at a predetermined time and amount over the course of the loan.

These arrangements can provide seniors with cash they need to live on. Often older people wind up house rich and cash poor. By getting a reverse mortgage, they can have both a regular source of income to meet expenses and a place to live until they die or are forced to move out of the house. The loan will generally not be repaid until the person dies or sells the house.

Many different financial institutions offer reverse mortgages. The *Department of Housing and Urban Development* (HUD) offers a list of approved lenders at **www.hud.gov/buying/reverse.cfm**. After finding a lending institution that does these kinds of loans, you will need to fill out an application. You must meet the lending institution's underwriting requirements. The person reviewing your application will look at such factors as interest rates, your age, and the value of the house in order to determine how much money they will lend you.

This loan has much of the complexities of a regular mortgage, so you should plan on it taking a fairly long time. Loans that are secured by real property require closings and many formalities that take time.

Even though this loan requires time and documentation, it has one main advantage. With a reverse mortgage, a senior gets to stay in his or her home, while at the same time using the home to raise cash for living expenses. In most cases, a secured debt, like a reverse mortgage, will also cost less in interest than many other debts.

The payout may come in several different ways. You might receive one large payment that you could use to payoff your other debts. You could also receive it in set monthly amounts or for a smaller amount every month, as long as you are alive and living in the house. You might be able to negotiate a combination of all three of these payments. That way you could have a partial lump sum payout as well as amount payment.

This is not a cheap or fast loan to acquire. All mortgages generate a lot of fees. This one is no exception. The other huge disadvantage is that if you need to tap the equity in your home again for any reason you will have already used it up. You can't borrow against the same equity twice. *Equity* is the difference between what you owe and what you own.

Another factor to consider with this loan is the effect it may have on your estate planning goals. For many people, their house is the significant asset that they may want to pass on to their children when they die. However a reverse mortgage alters the distribution of the house, because instead of being left to the heirs, the house would either have to be sold off to recover the amount of the loan or the heirs would have to pay off the loan before assuming title to the house.

Another area for concern is that financial transactions involving senior citizens have traditionally been ripe pickings for con artists. Like any kind of financial transaction involving your house, you need to be particularly wary of offers you don't initiate and offers that sound to good to be true. Offers of help with financing that come out of the blue from contractors are a particularly red flag. For example, you should be wary of the contractor who happens to be driving by and notices that your roof is bad and can help you out with financing the repairs.

Finally, this strategy requires tapping your home. Just like food, basic shelter is an imperative need. It also differs from a house sale. The sale ends any obligation to keep up the house or pay taxes. With this loan, the person living in the house still has to pay the real estate taxes and pay for the upkeep of the house. Because this loan can affect so many parts of your life, you should talk to your family financial advisers before committing to it.

Generally, loans do not qualify as income, so the reverse mortgage should not affect eligibility for most government programs. Nonetheless government eligibility rules may change and you may wish to check this before getting a reverse mortgage.

There are several resources anyone contemplating a reverse mortgage should be aware of. The *Federal Trade Commission* has very helpful material on their website at **www.ftc.gov**. In addition, the *Department of Housing and Urban Development* at **www.hud.gov** has very useful information. Finally, the *National Center for Home Equity Conversion,*

360 N Robert #403 Saint Paul MN 55101, 651-222-6775 as well as their website at **www.reverse.org/NCHEC.HTM** provides available amount information.

AARP is the nation's largest organization for people over fifty. They have a website that should be the first place to look for this issue and other issues that are of particular interest to people over fifty. The website can be found at **www.aarp.org**.

No Income/No Asset Loans

Anyone who needs quick cash and has real estate should also be aware of two other options. The no *income/no asset loan* is the kind of loan self-employed people can grow to love. If you are a self-employed person who doesn't have a stable source of income, it can be difficult to persuade a bank or other conventional mortgage lender to lend you money. However this is where this loan comes into play.

This loan essentially looks for things that a person in that category might have available, such as good credit and collateral in the form of real estate. In this case, cash flow doesn't figure into the loan, instead the loan is driven by the two other factors. The lending institution is using the credit score to reassure itself that based on the past history of paying bills, the person has both the money and the inclination to pay off the loan. Secondly, this is a mortgage. That means the lending institution now has a security interest in the house and may foreclose on it if the borrower defaults.

As with all loans, there are advantages and disadvantages to this loan. On the advantage side, it is cash and it is fast with about as little paperwork for a real estate mortgage as is possible. However, there are also significant drawbacks relative to conventional mortgages. First of all, you can expect to pay a much higher interested rate for the money. Because this is a riskier loan for the lender, it will cost more and have a higher interest rate. Secondly, these mortgages are often adjustable rate mortgages. This means the rate of interest is not fixed and may go up. Lastly, these are often *balloon mortgages*. That means that the payment balloons up and becomes due and payable. As a practical matter this means that the borrower will be forced to refinance the loan at possibly much higher rates.

Hard Money Mortgage Loans

Like the no income/no asset loan, this loan is for the person who has real estate, but needs cash. Small real estate entrepreneurs often have no recourse but to use hard money lenders to get the money to finance their project. The rates for these loans are apt to be significantly higher than those of banks. However, these lenders may give you the loan when the banks may just show you the door. They are almost purely collateral based. They also often have very short loan periods. It is a source of money and it can be the only source. But it is risky and has a high interest rate.

Hard money lenders for real estate can be found on the web. In addition, real estate groups may be able to put you in touch with them. For example, the *Chicago Creative Investors Association* and other groups have websites that may be able to help you. This website,

www.realestatepromo.com, has a listing of local real estate investor clubs. Another great website for resources on these kind of hard money loans and for a directory of real estate investor clubs is **www.real-estate-online.com/real-estate-clubs/il.html**. The clubs may be the highest quality source of information on creative financing for real estate around. The members are working in real estate and looking for creative ways to buy it and borrow against it.

Veterans Loans

Federal and state governments have created many unique programs for veterans. If you are a veteran, you may be eligible for a low interest loan from your state for veterans. There are certain qualifications that you must meet. Of course you must meet the veteran eligibility of some service in the United States military—usually at least ninety days. You must also be a resident of the state from where you are applying. These requirements are set by the state legislature.

The application for the loan can be acquired from the state veterans offices in your state. A listing of state veterans offices may be found on the web at **www.tvc.state.tx.us/States.htm**; at the national association web page at **www.nasdva.com**; and the federal Veterans Affairs office website is at **www.va.gov**

The loan application requires standard information, such as name, social security number, date of birth, address, how long at your present address, phone number, and email address.

State governments create these veteran loans programs. Your state government may or may not have created one. However, by contacting the state government switchboard, you should be able to reach the state veterans office. In general, any state or federal loan program is going to offer cheaper rates than private alternatives. The major disadvantage of federal and state loans is that it's going to take time. The other disadvantage is that federal and state loans will be credit score and cash flow based loans.

State and federal loan programs are creatures of the government. As such your elected official may be able to expedite the processing or otherwise help you with it.

These state loans are not to be confused with the federal veterans administration loans that can be used to purchase homes or refinance existing VA loans.

PAWN SHOPS

Other than borrowing from friends and family, pawn shops are probably the oldest way of raising cash in existence today. According to the old legend, Queen Isabella pawned the Spanish royal jewels so Columbus could have the cash to sail on his voyage of discovery to the New World in 1492.

The same basic principles that governed pawn arrangements then, still apply today. A pawnshop is a pure *collateral lender*. Some lenders care about cash flow, a very few care about your personal character, and many care about your credit score, but a pawnbroker is really only interested in one thing—collateral.

The collateral is whatever object you bring in to pawn. Objects run the gamut of consumer goods ranging from the exotic like a glass eye to fairly common items such as power tools and video games. Some items are particularly good candidates for pawning, such as tools, jewelry, personal electronics, and musical instruments. Although car title loans have their own section, some pawnshops take vehicles as well.

Many pawnshops are set up like banks with teller cages. Others are more like retail stores. Regardless of the physical layout, the transaction is much the same. You take the item or items you've picked out to pawn to the *pawnbroker*. The pawnbroker then looks at it and comes up with a price. To be successful, pawnbrokers have to have a very good feel for exactly what your item will sell for in the retail market. Many use collector's guides, their own experience, and online auctions to come up with a reasonable offer. Expect that the amount you are offered will be far below what you know the item to be worth. The loan process generates some money for pawnbrokers, but retail sales are a very significant part of their bottom line.

After the pawnbroker sets the price, he or she will give you a pawn ticket. The ticket will describe how much you pay to redeem the item and should disclose the effective interest rate on the loan as well. As a general rule, a pawnshop loan will be for a term of one to four months and have a very high interest rate. Some states cap the interest rate at 36%; others do not.

Pawning has several advantages and disadvantages. It is not a particularly cheap loan. In fact, it can be a very expensive loan. There is always the possibility that your item will be sold if you cannot redeem it. However, it could be a cheaper loan than the payday loans. Unlike payday loans that can be renewed several times, a pawnshop loan will end. After the loan period ends, you will either have paid if off or the pawnbroker will sell off the collateral.

Before pawning an item, you may wish to consider that perhaps an outright sale might work better. A pawnbroker has to loan you less than what they can sell the item for in order to make a profit. If the item is one you can sell and no longer need, then a direct sale might work better. However, this may take more time than using a pawnbroker when weighing all the factors of your decision.

CONSUMER FINANCE COMPANIES

Consumer finance companies have been around for a long time. They exist in a netherworld of finance between banks and pawnshops in terms of raising cash. They are loan companies that specialize in loaning small amounts of money to consumers who generally need it in a hurry. There is no one group of people who uses consumer finance companies. Their customers come from all classes, occupations, and income groups.

Consumer finance companies have more flexible lending rules than banks, but the actual application process is much like a bank. Either online, in person, or over the phone, you have to give them sufficient information to put your application through their loan application process.

Signature Loan

As a practical matter, the loan itself may be what is known as a *signature loan*. A signature loan is the purest form of a credit score and cash flow loan in existence. As discussed earlier, lending institutions look at the three Cs to decide if the borrower gets the money and how much he or she pays for it. *Cash flow* is simply the difference between the money you have coming in to pay bills and how much money is going out during the same period. The more money coming in relative to what is going out, the more likely the lending institution will be to approve the loan. *Collateral* is what you put up that the lending company can take and sell if you don't pay the loan off. For banks there is little money in being in the repo game, so they avoid making loans that require them to sell off the collateral.

This loan has no collateral attached to it. So it is a pure *credit score* and cash flow play. If the consumer finance company evaluates the application and the credit score is high enough, the employment or income history is long enough, the loan application will probably be approved. Borrowers need not have as high a credit rating as is usually demanded by other institutions. Several factors go into the consumer's credit scores, such as timeliness and the overall amount of credit the consumer has borrowed relative to their income. However, for a personal loan that is not secured by collateral, it is hard to overestimate how important the person's credit score will be in getting the loan.

Consumer finance companies can be can be found in the Yellow Pages or on the web. In addition, they often advertise in the local penny saver or free want ad papers. Although a loan from a consumer finance company may be faster than a bank, you should still think in terms of weeks, not days.

Risk vs Reward

Some consumer finance companies have a better handle on the art of lending smaller amounts to consumers than do other financial institutions. Not only are they able to make small cash loans to consumers, but they are often more willing. These companies have been serving this market since the early years of the last century. They have a lot of experience and are more willing than banks to over look problems with the three Cs. For example, consumer finance companies may accept credit histories that have a few bangs and dents. They will also generally be willing to look at credit scores and credit histories that are less than perfect.

Imagine that all loans are a teeter-totter with risk on one end and reward on another. The more risk that a lender takes, the more reward *(interest)* the lender is going to want in return. These institutions exist somewhere between pawnshops and banks because they are willing to take more risk than banks, but not as many as pawnshops. Consumer finance companies will reject applicants who pose too great a risk. Pawnshops will generally loan out to anybody, so long as the property is not stolen.

This willingness to take risks comes at a price to the borrower. Borrowers should expect to get the lowest interest rates from family, then life insurance loans, then credit unions, then banks, then consumer finance companies, then credit card advances then pawnshops, car title loans, and finally loan sharks. So borrowers can definitely expect to pay more than they would at banks—assuming the bank is willing to lend to them.

Insurance

Consumer finance companies know that if the borrower gets sick or dies they will be a very low priority bill. Since they also know they have no collateral like a house or car to sell to recover their money, they have to protect their money somehow. So, these lenders may require borrowers to purchase something called *credit life* or *disability insurance* along with this type of loan. Consumer finance companies are particularly likely to require borrowers to buy this insurance. This kind of insurance indirectly protects the borrower. It's really designed to protect the consumer finance company in case the borrower can't work or dies. The premiums for this insurance get merged into the borrower's monthly payments.

Like other loans that depend heavily on cash flow and credit scores, this one has to be arranged before the need the critical cash crunch time. Even though the loans may be available to people with lower credit scores, finance companies won't lend after the credit score goes down to far because of unpaid bills or after job loss.

Consumer finance companies are very much regulated entities. Both federal and state governments may monitor their activity. In particular, consumers should pay close attention to the *Truth in Lending* law that requires lenders to disclose how much the finance charges are and how much the *APR* or *annual percentage rate* will be.

LIFE INSURANCE

In a real sense, loans against your life insurance policies are loans you take out from yourself. Depending on the type of life insurance you have, it may have a *cash value* that you can borrow against or take out. The cash value is part of the money that you have paid into the insurance company in the form of *premiums* throughout the years. *Whole life* policies and *universal life* policies can carry a cash, which can be borrowed against. However, much life insurance is what is known as *term*. Term insurance is like the kind on your house or car, and it has no cash value. You cannot borrow against a term life insurance policy.

You should easily be able to find this information by contacting your insurance company on its website or 800 number, or by calling your agent. This loan should go fairly quickly in comparison to other types of loans. For example, a mortgage on real estate involves closings and title searches as well as credit reports. Personal loans involve the application and credit reports. This loan should basically be between you and the insurance company.

The big advantage is that this can be cheap and readily easy money to acquire. The insurance company will be an easy creditor. If you pay them back, that's great and if you don't, the only loss is yourself. In the end, the money will come out of the proceeds of the insurance policies.

The disadvantage with this policy is if your beneficiary turns out to really need the money, he or she will be in for a rude awakening. If the policy has a cash value and you borrow most of it, that could greatly diminish the financial cushion you wanted to provide for your loved ones. Always remember most people have less insurance than they think they do. If you really were using insurance for its purpose of replacing income lost because of an untimely death, the death benefit is going to be used up pretty fast.

This transaction should go fairly easily and quickly. If it does not, remember that insurance is one of the most regulated industries in existence. If you have any suspicions that you've been treated unfairly or improperly and your efforts to resolve them with the company have not met with success, every state has an office of state government responsible for regulating insurance companies.

401(K) ACCOUNTS

401(k) refers to the section of the U.S. tax code that authorizes the creation of an *employee deferred tax investment plan*. These plans allow employees to invest in their retirement on a tax-deferred basis. This means that the employee investor does not get taxed on the money until there is a distribution of the income and principal.

The plan generally contemplates that the money will be given to the employee when he or she reaches retirement and leaves the employment of the company. A 403(b) plan is the 401(k) equivalent for not for profit companies.

The actual loan is made on the form that the administrator of the plan supplies or the plan website should have a copy of the form to request a loan. This is a relatively fast and quick procedure. Think in terms of weeks not months.

A big advantage is that you're borrowing the money from yourself, so you'll be certain that the loan will be approved. The other advantage is that you'll be borrowing against something that you already own. Because it is a regulated loan and one secured by your own assets, expect a fairly low to moderate interest rate. The interest rate should be around the *prime rate*, plus or minus a couple of points. There is also an early withdrawal penalty of 10%

The biggest disadvantage is the effect it could have on your retirement. Even though the cash crunch is urgent, by taking money out of this account you are lowering the amount that will be available when you retire. By taking the money out early, you are not only interrupting its growth (hopefully) but you are also risking paying tax on it. This defeats the purpose of the 401(k) since the money is supposed to be left in place to grow tax deferred.

Unlike a loan from an insurance company, you will probably have to repay this sooner or later. If you voluntarily leave your job, are fired, or downsized, it could be sooner as your now former employer, in most cases, will require that you pay the money back or pay the penalties on an early withdrawal.

A 401(k) has special federal income tax characteristics and advantages so the Internal Revenue Code actually controls loans against the value of a 401(k). However as a practical matter, the human resources department of your company should be able to offer you guidance and assistance. You will need to repay money borrowed against a 401(k), because if you don't, the tax penalties can be severe.

BROKERAGE ACCOUNTS

Brokerage accounts are accounts people have with stock brokers and investment houses. The accounts can take many forms ranging from shares of companies, mutual funds, commodities, or bond funds. There may be significant advantages to borrowing against them for quick cash, rather than selling them.

If the assets are sold, then they can be subject to *capital gains* on the profit if they have been held for a long enough time. If they have been held for a shorter period, they may not qualify for capital gains rates (which are generally lower) and may be taxed at a higher income tax rate.

Borrowing money usually requires credit scores, cash flow, and collateral in a very specific mix for banks. Other institutions willing to lend money may view the mix differently. Elements that are very important to one lender may not matter much at all to another lender. Such is the case with these loans. Think of this as a Wall Street version of a pawnshop loan. Looked at from the lenders perspective this is a very good deal. The broker knows you own the stock. He or she knows exactly what the stock is likely worth and how to sell it if you don't pay. Just as pawnbrokers are really in the retail business, brokers are not really in the lending business—they are in the business of selling stock and other securities.

To set this loan up, you sign a form with your broker and agree to pay the loan back at a certain amount of interest. If you don't pay, they take your stock and sell it. Nothing could be simpler. They already have possession of the stock and are in the business of selling stock, so from their end of the deal it's a pretty simple transaction.

However there are certain restrictions. Just as the pawnshop does not intend to lend good money on junk consumer goods, neither does the Wall Street company have any intention of loaning good money on bad stock. Brokerage houses are only interested in things they can sell easily and quickly if you default, so some investments will not work for a loan. For example IRAs, 401(k)s and educational IRAs are bad bets. Further, the securities you are putting up for the loan have to be traded on a large stock exchange, such as the New York or American Stock Exchanges or the NASDAQ.

Penny Stocks

Penny stocks are highly speculative stocks that sell for less than a dollar on very small exchanges. They would be a very bad source of a loan.

For a stock to be taken seriously, it usually has to trade for at least ten dollars a share. So as a rule of thumb, do not expect to borrow money on a stock trading for less than ten dollars a share.

Margin Loans

These kinds of loans are different from traditional *margin loans*. A traditional margin loan is where a person borrows money to buy stock, by using stock they already own as a collateral. These loans are not for investment purposes. Investment purpose margin loans are highly regulated by the SEC.

The loans can either be paid back at a date set in the future or can start making installment payments right away. You may be able to borrow on a couple of your accounts at the same time.

Line of Credit

If you have enough cash flow right now but are worried about the future, you might want to think about getting a line of credit loan on your securities. The downside is that the interest rate might not be fixed. The good thing is that you would have the money when you needed it.

Since this is a strictly collateral pay loan, your ability to meet the cash flow requirements of paying the loan back should not matter as much as it would to a bank. Nevertheless, it is always easier to borrow money when you don't need it. This way you could draw on the money when you needed it.

As a general rule, expect this kind of loan to have far fewer fees and hassles than other types of collateral loans, such as mortgages, car title loans, or pawnshops. Also expect a lower rate of interest than many of the other types. For example, on a fixed rate the interest rate would be tied to the prime rate and set for the life of the loan. On a revolving line of credit loan, it would vary and move up and down with the prime rate. One big advantage of this loan is that you should be able to avoid all of the lending fees that come with mortgaging real estate, such as points, application fees, appraisals, and prepayment penalties.

PENSION ACCOUNTS

Pensions are not nearly as easy to get money out of as some other investment alternatives. For example, borrowing cash against a life insurance policy is very easy and fast. Borrowing against a 401(k) is also comparatively fast and easy. Pensions are not.

If you can qualify for early retirement, you might have an easier time getting to the money. However, this is not really a good strategy if you just need a comparatively little amount of cash. Pensions are very complex financial entities. There are many investment and tax considerations that go into setting up a pension plan. These considerations usually make it largely impossible for the average person to raise cash using his or her pension.

However, there is one very important exception well worth looking into if you need cash quickly. If you have only been with the company for a short period of time and you separate from them, you may be able to get the value of the pension in cash, early. The value has to be less than $5,000, and there could be tax consequences. You should discuss this with your financial advisor before using this method to raise quick cash.

CASH ADVANCES

Credit cards are everywhere and they can definitely be a source of quick cash in the form of a *cash advance*. Cash advances can be obtained at ATMs or by using checks supplied by the credit card companies at banks. Also, the credit card companies have provisions for obtaining emergency cash advance services if you're traveling and have all your valuables disappear.

Credit cards differ in that they go by *credit* or *charge cards*. *Charge cards* are supposed to be paid off at the end of the month. Credit cards on the other hand, allow balances to accumulate and be charged interest. While standard credit card rates are about 15% and up, cash advance can go from 20% and up.

The main advantage of this strategy is that it's so fast and easy. Go to an ATM, insert the card, enter your PIN, out comes the cash. Many small business owners who know they will never get financing any other way, get ten credit cards and get $1,000 cash advances to come up with the $10,000 they figure they need to get going. It's not cheap money and you have to have credit that's good enough to qualify, but it's definitely one way to raise cash.

Once you are done adding up the fees to get the cash advance, the high credit card interest rates, and the possible ATM fees, you've got one very high priced source of quick cash. Pay careful attention to exactly what fees your credit card company charges. For instance, some charge a percentage of the transaction, others charge a flat fee. Many charge both for a combined fee.

The other thing to remember is that some credit card transactions have a *grace period* in which you can pay them off without interest or penalties. There is generally no such period for the cash advance.

Also credit card companies apply your payment in an order they prescribe. They may apply your payments to the other debt you have on the card before they pay off any of the cash advance. So it you can't pay off the whole balance, you may wind up paying the higher interest rate on the whole balance you're carrying. Only if you don't have any other debt on the card and you're sure you can pay off the whole balance within the month are these good sources of quick cash.

Sell It

5

This is by far one of the best options. Now is the time to get rid of things you've been hanging on to without a clear purpose or an attachment. There are many advantages to this strategy. By selling off property you already own, you can accomplish two things. You can create space by getting rid of clutter and you can raise the cash you need without going into debt.

Collectibles and antiques are huge right now. *Antiques Roadshow* is the most popular TV show on PBS. There has never been a better or easier time to convert property into liquid cash. eBay's volume is in the millions. Plus, the majority of eBay items sell for fewer than $20, so chances are the average person has more money laying around than he or she thinks.

However, before cashing some things in or selling off your things, keep a few things in mind. First and foremost, do not sell something you don't own and have clear title to. Secondly, make sure there is no outside factor preventing you from selling it without permission.

Certain proceedings generate estates. *Estate* is a legal term that means the extent of a person's real and personal property. *Real property* means property such as land and houses. There are *probate estates, martial estates,* and *bankruptcy estates.* These are collections of property belonging to people who have died or are getting divorced or are going through a bankruptcy. You may feel the property you want to sell to raise cash is yours free and clear, but if the property belonged to a deceased relative whose estate is still open or either of the other two cases, don't even think of selling it unless you check with a lawyer first.

Generally speaking, if you own the object, you can sell it to raise cash if you want to. Of all the possible ideas for raising cash, this may be one of the best, and it's never been easier. The advantages are huge. You already own it, so you don't have to borrow money. Since you are not borrowing, you are not going further into debt, risking losing your house or car. And, if you choose it right, you may be able to solve your cash flow and get rid of junk you neither want nor need any more.

There are many different ways of selling stuff that are determined mostly by what kind of stuff you have to sell. This section is limited to what most people have that consists of personal property. Legally, anything that isn't considered an interest in real property is *personal property*. From a practical perspective, personal property means the stuff most of us are living with. This wide range of objects varies enormously from person to person, so this is a general discussion with guides and references included to help with questions about more specific areas.

When you're on the selling end of the deal, you need to make some hard decisions going into it. This principal applies whether you are selling the Renoir you were fortunate to inherit or Uncle Larry's shot glass collection that has been collecting dust in the attic for six years. First off, you must absolutely do your best to find out the fair market value of the object. Second, you have to make your mind up that a good deal for the buyer is not necessarily a bad deal for you. For example, in Illinois many dealers and regular folks buy antiques at country auctions located in towns miles away from Chicago. The rule of thumb was that for every fifty miles closer to Chicago the antique got, the price would double until it arrived for sale in the City. So a chair that someone bought for $50 one-hundred miles from Chicago would double and then double again so it should sell for $200 by the time it arrived in the city. And, of course, the antique might change hands several times before it winds up in an exclusive shop in Chicago.

All of this greatly affects how much a dealer can afford to pay you for what you are selling. If you have the ability to sell the table yourself for close to the retail price or if you are very much attached to it, then it might be a very bad deal. On the other hand, you may hate the table, and have no way to sell it yourself. In that case, any offer that was not ridiculously low would be a good deal. The key in this example, and really in all examples, is to do your homework so you have a pretty accurate idea of what the item is worth. However, if you are selling to dealers, you have to appreciate that you cannot get retail prices from what is essentially a wholesale transaction. The dealer has to make a living as well.

EXAMPLE: Many book dealers pay people to find rare books for them at thrift stores and auctions. If the book dealer pays a book picker ten dollars for a book, but sells it for $150, that may still be a good deal for the book picker. Without the help of the book dealer, the picker might not have known the contacts it would be necessary to find a willing buyer.

Doing your homework and the necessary research is the key. It gives you some control over the process of selling things to raise cash. Check out the guide books and the retail shops where your items could be sold. Always figure that the person you are selling to knows exactly how much its worth. Knowing the value of your property can give you options. Once you know what the item is potentially worth, you will spot a good deal or decide to explore other options such as putting the item on eBay or listing it in the want ads.

The other factor you have to consider in all of your research is that what you are selling is probably not an item people *have* to buy at any price. Therefore, your ability to sell an item may come down to timing. Sure there are examples of people who would sell the clothes off of their back for the hottest collectible, but those examples are rare. A sale depends on a willing buyer and a willing seller, who settle at an agreed upon price. So for example, at a real physical auction, if the crowd is dead for a certain item, the item will not bring what the guidebooks say it might. On the other hand, if a mediocre item catches the eye of two people who just have to have it, the sky's the limit.

Another factor you may want to consider with the sale of items is that unlike borrowing, selling items can cause tax implications. In general, borrowing money will not cause your income to rise for tax purposes. However, selling items generally will count as *ordinary income*, so potentially it could affect your tax liability for federal, state, and local taxes if they apply to income where you live.

ANTIQUES AND COLLECTIBLES

The *antique* industry defines antiques as *items that were made at least one hundred years ago. Collectibles* is a term used for *items less than one hundred years old.* Collectibles are valuable because of their unique beauty or because they are a mass-produced item people want to collect. People who like to collect often blur the distinctions.

If you need to raise cash, these could well be the solution to your problem. For example, the success of the free appraisal show, *Antiques Roadshow,* has greatly increased the accessibility and interest in this information. In addition, the Kovel's have built an empire on getting the word out on antique and collectible values. Kovel's guide to antiques and collectibles can be found online at **www.kovels.com**.

If you're in need of cash, this is definitely one of the first places you should look. Plus, with the advent of eBay and other electronic trading platforms it has truly never been easier to turn your treasures into cash treasures.

Many things people would never consider collectible can actually be quite good sources of quick cash. For example, a whole publication exists devoted to collecting old video games (*Digital Press Collector's Guide* at **www.digitalpress.com**). Just as *Kelley's Blue Book* is a guide to selling your car or *Kovel's* antique guides are the mainstay of antiques, this guide serves as a guide to how much your vintage Atari may bring.

However, selling antiques has always been a risky endeavor for the nondealer seller. All of those fabulous stories of the piece of rare Chippendale furniture being sold by the farmer who had it back in the barn for years before selling it for $100—all start with the buyer who knew more about the object than the owner. In this case, you'll be the seller so you definitely want to know what it is worth. Because whether you sell it by Internet auction, physical auction, classified, yard sale, or from the back of your car, once it's gone it's gone.

You must also know whether you will be causing yourself any legal problems by selling it. There are most definitely some antiques and collectibles that are better left alone. For example, some old stuffed birds are protected under the federal *Migratory Bird Act of 1918*. This Act makes it a criminal offense to sell certain birds stuffed and mounted after the Act.

In addition, firearms and ammunition present special issues. First of all keep them well away from children and people who might handle them carelessly. Secondly be sure you contact local law enforcement BEFORE you move them or try to sell them. You don't want to violate any laws you don't know about. Native American art and artifacts also have special rules and regulations attached to their sale. Last but not least, it goes without saying, do not sell anything you don't have the right to sell. For a full listing of items, including many antiques and collectibles that may cause you problems if you sell them, see Appendix D.

Dangers of Cleaning Up Antiques and Collectibles

NOTE: *DO NOT WASH, POLISH, CLEAN, REFURBISH, OR REFINISH ANTIQUES AND COLLECTIBLES IF THEY APPEAR TO BE TRULY OLD.*

Although it seems strange since new things only sell if they are clean, antiques are the opposite. Books that would be worth hundreds of dollars with the faded book jacket on, may only be worth less than $10 without it. Furniture that could have been worth thousands may only be worth hundreds if it is refinished or cleaned improperly. The same thing goes for coins. Don't take the chance of cleaning it up until you are sure you know what it's worth.

Another factor that applies to the value of antiques and collectibles is what collectors call *provenance*—it is a fancy word that means history. For example, if it was known that George Washington stayed in a particular house during the Battle of Princeton and a map of the battlefield was found there, that would only help authenticate its story and make it more valuable. Another example is that old toys with the original packaging are worth much more than just the toys.

Selling

As for the nuts and bolts of how antiques or collectibles are actually sold—it depends.

Internet

Many people use eBay and other auctions to sell them. Basically, an antique is listed for sale in much the same way as any other item for sale. If you're certain you want to raise cash selling antiques online, see the Kovel's guide to selling antiques or collectibles online at **www.kovels.com**. It is specially designed to assist the beginning online antique seller.

Another unique resource that you might want to explore is *The Internet Antique Store* (TIAS). This is a wonderful resource for anyone learning about the world of antiques. It is an Internet service that allows people to sell their antiques online for a fee. It is not an auction. Instead it works like an Internet store with fixed prices. If you have a lot of stuff to sell, it might be well worth your while to set up a site. If not, it's still a great way to look at a broad section of items to help discover the possible value of what you might have.

However, if the thought of even putting the first little toe of your foot on to the electronic superhighway of the Internet leaves you dismayed, don't despair. There are still quite a few ways to turn antiques into quick cash.

Antique Malls

In the last number of years, many parts of the country have seen a boom in antique malls. An antique mall is a group of antique sellers and dealers organized around a common building. There are several advantages for them and for buyers. They get to split the costs of having a store between them, so it is not so formidable. Shoppers browse many different collections by going to one central location. This may benefit you in two different ways. First you may be able to shop your item to dealers if they are there to see what they would pay you for it. There is a risk to selling to dealers in that they are unlikely to give you what an excited individual bidder would pay for your treasure on eBay or at a physical auction. On the other hand, they are in the business of constantly buying and selling inventory.

The other strategy you might want to pursue is to ask the dealer if he or she will sell the item on consignment for you. *Consignment* is an arrangement where you deposit your antique or collectible with a dealer but the dealer doesn't own the item until he or she sells it to the customer. Then, the dealer pays you back the price he or she got for it minus his or her fee for selling it. If this works, this can be a win-win for you and the dealer. You want to raise cash not be in the antique business, so it works for you by saving you time and trouble. For the dealer, he or she can bolster up his or her inventory of interesting pieces to use to get customers into the store.

Like any strategy that involves you entrusting your personal property into the hands of someone you don't know, there are also profound dangers you should watch out for. First, always get the consignment agreement in a writing that simply, but completely, spells out what exactly is going to happen. It should explain what is happening; who the parties are; how much the dealer's commission is; what duty the dealer has to care for the piece; whether the dealer carries insurance for loss; and, what provisions you have to recover is there is a theft, bankruptcy, or fire. You should also make sure the dealer discloses if there is any likelihood his or her inventory will be attached by any other creditor. The last thing you want to be doing is fighting with some bank three states away over whether the dealer or you actually own Aunt Mildred's table.

Second, fully document the transaction from your end. This means you should take a picture of your item. Video is better so you can describe it thoroughly for the record, including all the identifying marks.

Flea Markets

Selling antiques and collectibles at a *flea market* might be an option for you if you can meet certain requirements. First, you have to be absolutely certain that within the time frame that you needed the cash you could recover all of your fees for getting a booth and any other fees associated with selling. Flea markets are great fun. They offer great street theatre and some wonderful bargains, as well as the opportunity to get outside. What they may offer you as a seller is a lot of work you don't need if you just want to raise a couple of hundred dollars. On the other hand you may love it. But you should be aware that selling items at flea markets are very much a regulated activity that falls under all applicable state and local laws, including sales tax and business licenses.

ONLINE SITES

Online auctions offer wonderful possibilities for people in search of quick cash. Think of eBay as the garage sale that never ends or the flea market that you never have to sit on the asphalt to sell at. Online auctions put your collectibles in front of a huge audience that will appreciate them and pay for them. If you have a garage sale, you're limited to who drives over. If you go to a flea market, you're limited to who comes by. But online, you can put your wares in front of a whole electronic community.

However, just as there are perils in selling items at a garage sale, there are perils in the electronic auctions as well. One of the most prevalent risks on electronic auctions is that sellers will not be paid. So, the preventative measure is to get paid before shipping the item. Another peril that must be guarded against is *identity theft*. The threat is real and precautions must be taken.

Yet, for all of the real dangers involved in Internet auctions, eBay and its rivals Yahoo.com and Amazon.com offer some of the best possible ways to raise cash quickly without a lot of cost. The advantages are huge and the risks are relatively small. This could be the ticket to turning clutter into cash on a modest or a massive scale.

eBay

eBay is the largest person-to-person online trading community that there has ever been. When you think of the volume of objects listed on eBay—think millions. The diversity of items listed for sale runs from Pez dispensers to tractors. Granted most of eBay's transactions are fewer than $20, but there are certainly many that garner far more. Plus, how much cash you need to raise is very much a relative thing. If you made fifty sales of $20 a piece in a month, the extra thousand dollars or so might be all the quick cash you need.

An eBay auction usually takes a week, but by making different choices in how the item is listed, it might be sold within minutes. Plus, with an electronic payment mechanism, you may have the money within hours, if not minutes, of the end of the auction. It's hard not to view this as one of the best options around for raising cash quickly.

Of course, everything this bright with possibility also casts quite a shadow. In the case of eBay and other Internet commerce sites, there are some pretty vile things in those shadows. For example, the Federal Trade Commission has targeted Internet auction as one of the leading sources of consumer fraud into the U.S. Plus, identity thieves routinely target eBay users (among others) with false emails designed to lure people into disclosing their social security number and other personal information that can be used for identity theft.

In addition, some people just do not want to be bothered. Doing eBay on a big scale is work. It can quickly become more like running a small curio and relic store than having a hobby. However, by following the basics described, you shouldn't have too many problems.

NOTE: *The steps listed are for the average person who has a need to raise cash quickly. There are whole books written telling people how to make their livings off of eBay. This is not that guide.*

Selling on eBay

The first thing you need to sell things on eBay is access to the World Wide Web so you can visit the site at **www.eBay.com**. Unlike garage sales and flea markets, eBay's great advantage is that you can do it from the comfort and privacy of your own home. Try selling your collection of cartoon salt and pepper shakers at the local antique mall at 3:00 a.m. on a Saturday night and you'll quickly realize one of eBay's main advantages. eBay runs 24 hours a day, 365 days a year. So if you want to sell your collectibles in your slippers without leaving your home office, eBay is a great option.

Of course, this assumes you have a computer and Internet connection at home. If you don't, there are several possibilities. You can borrow a friend or relatives. Libraries have computers. Kinko's has them. You can connect to the Web through cable TV and you may be able to do it at work. You should carefully review your office's Internet and computer usage policy before you decide to do it at work. Many companies routinely monitor their employees' email and Internet activity. Nobody wants to get in trouble or worse, fired, for having too successful an eBay empire.

Assuming you've made the leap online, the absolute best way to figure out eBay is to log onto the site at **www.eBay.com**. The eBay people have had a long time to perfect materials designed to simply and easily explain how to set up an account to buy and sell.

To use eBay, you must register and get an eBay account name. Do not use your email address as your account name. Everyday spammers troll through eBay harvesting email addresses to *spam*. Don't be one of the people who winds up as a target for junk email or identity theft. In fact, eBay will soon be phasing out the use of email addresses to help prevent these abuses. You will also need a credit card since it facilitates eBay's collection of fees.

You should be aware from the very beginning of two things as you get ready to list your item. First eBay is a for-profit venture. You pay a percentage of the auction and the value of the item to list your item on eBay. Then you pay more for the various refinements that you can add to the listing.

Secondly, you should absolutely know that eBay is an *auction*. You must know about what your item is worth before you list it because you will have to come up with a beginning price. This is crucial, be sure to get a good idea of what your item might be worth and pay very careful attention to how you list it and in what category. An auction is only interesting for the seller if there are two bidders—otherwise it's too likely to wind up as a low sale. (If you want to sell at a fixed price instead or even have a store on eBay, there are options to do that and you should explore them. This section is geared more for the person who wants to use eBay just to quickly raise cash with minimum investment of time and money.)

A host of services exist on and for eBay that can be used to make selling a large number of items easy. They may or may not interest you at this point. If you have a whole house full of things that you would love to get rid of on eBay, then this may be exactly what you need. Some of the specific items are helpful in setting up *merchant accounts* so you can accept credit cards in payment. Another helpful item is software that will allow you to manage your listings more efficiently. With the software, you can list items faster and you can choose what time of day you want to list them. Timing as discussed earlier is a crucial variable for some items.

Determining the Value of an Item

There are several ways you can find out what your stuff is worth. The easiest is to search eBay's past auction for similar items. Pay attention to the item, its condition, and opening bid. Other source of prices for your stuff is simply to seek it out wherever similar items are sold. If it is an antique waffle iron, go where the antique waffle irons are sold—flea markets, real people auctions, garages sales, and specialty antique sites such as **www.tias.com**. In addition, if it is an antique and it's being sold, there is a price guide for it. Most people who dabble in antiques have seen Kovel's guides to antiques or others like it. There's even one of antique video games—*Digital Press Collector's Guide*. Most people would think of baseball cards as a known collectible, and they'd be right, but it would be foolish to overlook a collection of old video games. Some can sell for thousands of dollars.

If all else fails, seek out an appraiser or try the *Antiques Roadshow* or check eBay's *inside scoop*. However, bear in mind that there is no price guide, website, or person who can really tell you exactly what your bauble is worth. Only a willing buyer and a willing seller can truly determine the worth of any item. Do not think of this as ways to absolutely guarantee the sale. Instead, think of it as a way not to sell a $500 item for $5.

One option you should very much be aware of is the chance to use a *reserve price* on your item. This means you can set a price, that unless you get that as a minimum, you will not have to sell the item.

Time Schedule

A crucial thing to understand about eBay is that it operates on its own time schedule. The eBay world is set to Pacific Standard Time. Unless you get the enhanced software, your item will be listed and your auction will start whenever you list the item. Depending on what you are trying to sell, this can be a very important factor. It you're listing a night owl nightshirt that appeals to the graveyard shift and you list it so the auction closes at 9:00 a.m. you'll probably miss them because they will be in bed. Likewise, if you decide to list your really cool corporate gizmo item but have the auction begin and end on Saturday morning at 3:00 a.m., your auction is not going to do as well as it could if it were set to a time that more of the 9-to-5 crowd could see it.

Fees

A brief rundown of eBay fees is as follows. eBay does its fees by what the item may bring. Any listing of fees should be checked against the website for accuracy, but eBay fees for listing an item are fairly modest. They start at thirty cents an item and go up to $3.30. Motorcycles are $25 and cars are $40 to list. In addition, there are other fees for various services that eBay offers that can make your listing more attractive.

Items to Sell

More so than any other option, eBay offers you the chance to dispose of more stuff and different stuff for cash quickly. For example, say you have an old laser disc player, if you put it out at your garage sale you'll be lucky to get $5 for it. Put it on eBay and you could clean up and have someone buy it for $100 or more.

Some ideas of what you could sell on eBay are as follows: antiques and collectibles, computers and software, old electronic equipment, books, and last year's Christmas and Hanukkah presents that you hated. In addition, eBay is a great way to get rid of unused home items like lamps, vases, pictures, and other knick knacks.

Even though eBay offers a great option for raising cash quickly there are limitations you might want to consider. Although people buy cars, tractors, and furniture on eBay, it seems to work easiest for small things that ship easily. This makes it a natural for small collectibles, such as baseball cards and glassware. It's also not particularly easy for some things like plain Jane kid clothes that would sell easily at a garage sale. One of the advantages of a garage sale is you can haggle and bundle up the stuff so you can get rid of it. eBay doesn't really lend itself to that. Plus, even if you could sell your kids old clothes for a quarter on eBay, would you really want to go all the trouble?

eBay also imposes several rules. Some of the rules are the result of U.S. laws and others are just the way eBay works. For example, it is a serious felony to sell child pornography anywhere in the U.S. Also, sales of firearms and war souvenirs such as artillery pikes and the like are subject to many restrictions. eBay just does not allow them.

In addition, sale of stuffed birds is prohibited on eBay just as it is outside of online trading platforms. You cannot sell something that infringes on someone's copyright, trademark, or patent.

You also cannot sell badges or replicas of official identification card or other papers related to identity such as birth certificates. Further, shipping regulations can make selling a particular item on eBay not a good idea. Several items cannot be shipped through the U.S. mail such as obscene materials, alcohol, and locksmithing tools.

Getting Paid

The most interesting part of eBay is, of course, how you get paid. First the auction ends and one person emerges victorious. When you list your item, you determine how you wish to get paid. For example, you may choose to only be paid by money order or you may branch out to the point that you are accepting credit cards.

If you take electronic payment like credit cards or *PayPal,* then there are some requirements you should be aware of. The eBay software will guide buyers through the transaction so that he or she can pay you. However, he or she must have a PayPal account to use it. This is an electronic web-based procedure that allows the buyer to send you an electronic check via email drawn off of his or her credit card. It greatly speeds up e-commerce on eBay and if you're going to use it a lot, its well worth the trouble.

NOTE: *One point cannot be emphasized enough, never pay for shipping and never ship until you have the buyer's payment firmly in hand.*

However, if you just want to make a brief foray into e-commerce for the limited purpose of raising cash fast, then you probably won't want to go to the trouble of exploring commercial merchant accounts and all the other bells and whistles. However one thing you can do that will make it easier for you to accept payments is to set up a PayPal account at **www.paypal.com**. PayPal is a financial intermediary service. It allows you to accept payment electronically instead of relying on money orders, cashier's checks, and personal checks. With PayPal you get the money fast. With the option of checks, you have to wait for them to be sent through the mail and then you have to deposit them.

In the hustle and bustle of raising money on eBay, it's important to remember that the vast majority of eBay transactions are between individuals and for less than $20. It pays to be nice. It also pays to ship promptly, to deliver what you promised, and to give and receive *feedback* carefully. Feedback is very important because it indicates what kind of seller you are.

Security

eBay also has several other safeguards that would-be sellers should know about. eBay's website at **http://pages.eBay.com/securitycenter** has several pages devoted to security issues for buyers and sellers. The section has very good practical suggestions for how to sell safely.

For further security, eBay offers *Square Trade*, an online dispute resolution service. eBay also offers defrauded sellers the opportunity to file a *nonpaying bidder alert*. This will allow the seller to get a *final value fee credit*—a one-time fee eBay charges on items it sells.

As a last resort, the FBI and several partners have set up an *Internet Fraud Complaint Center* at **www.ifccfbi.gov/strategy/fraudtips.asp**. This site allows people to learn about fraud on the Internet and to file complaints.

Half.com

Half.com is another online trading company—at least for now. It began as an independent venture, but is now owned by eBay. eBay has announced plans to integrate it fully into its own site. When it started, it offered a truly unique concept. The half referred to the idea that a person should be able to sell their book, CDs, or other stuff for about half what they paid for it.

Like *eBay* and *yahoo, half.com* has numerous resources to make it easier to electronically list items on its trading platform, but here's a crucial difference that can make listing items much faster. *Half.com* allows you to use bar codes such as the UPC and ISBN numbers to list items easily and quickly. This is a big advantage if you're listing something like books.

There is a crucial difference between eBay and half.com. eBay is an auction. Auctions have beginnings and endings. Half.com is more like an electronic consignment shop. You can post your listing and leave it there for a long time. When you list the item, if you're happy with the price, that's the price that it's going to keep throughout the listing until someone buys it or the listing eventually expires.

Listing on half.com can go very quickly—think minutes not hours. If it's a hot CD or book, it can move off very quickly. Of course, if it's overpriced, not in demand, or not in great shape, then it will take much longer to move.

Half.com is perfect for the person with a million books and CDs but doesn't want to put them on eBay because while they're in demand, they aren't special enough to really cause an all out bidding war. As an example, a used copy of a New York Times hardcover bestseller you're willing to sell for $7.00 may be a very good thing to list on half.com. The main disadvantage is it is a fixed price environment. If the item could ignite a bidding frenzy, then half.com is not the best place to list it.

Now that eBay has acquired half.com, many of its rules and regulations are much the same but there have been announcements that the site as well as its pricing may go away. Half.com listings lasted for a very long time—basically until someone bought the item. But in return for that, half.com took a hefty commission on the sale of the item, but no listing fee. For example, half.com took a 15% commission for items under $50 all the way down to a 5% commission for items $500 and above.

Dangers on all Internet Auction Sites

The Internet is a marvelous place to sell your stuff. Where else could you sell so many items for so much more than they would bring at a garage sale? The same item that would bring pennies at a garage sale, may bring dollars on eBay. In fact, many eBayers go to garage sales to get their inventories.

However, electronic auctions are like regular auctions in many ways. The phrase *watering stock* had its origins in the 1900s, when unscrupulous cattle drovers would give their cattle salted feed before they brought them into be weighed for sale. The cattle would then get thirsty and the drovers would let them drink to their fill. If the timing worked out, the cattle would be sold before nature took its course and the buyer would be stuck paying for worthless pounds of water instead of beef. The same motivations are still found on today's auctions.

Here are some things you should know to be sure your attempts to raise quick cash do not wind up costing you money in the long run. This section looks at it from the perspective of the person doing the selling since most people who want to use the Internet to raise cash will be selling off some of their stuff.

SELL IT • 119

One way people can take advantage of a buyer is a variation of a technique that has been used by unscrupulous people at a physical auction. This involves two bidders who work together to put in a real bid that is very low and then another bid that is very high. The high bid serves to discourage other people from bidding on the item, but it will be taken back towards the end of the auction and only the low bidder will remain. Once the auction is over, the poor seller will be left with a price that is far lower than what his or her item would have bought. If this happens to you, cancel the auction before it ends. Warning signs you might want to look for are new bidders with very low feedback points or bidders with bad feedback.

Another scheme you should watch is also an online variation of one that has existed in the real world for years. In this one, you agree to decide that you are going to raise cash by selling off an old car, but the car, for whatever reason, will not bring as much money locally as it would if you could list it to a much wider audience. So you decide to list online. All goes well with listing the car, there seems to be interest, and quite a few bidders are bidding. Finally the auction ends with a winner who gets the car for a closing price of $6000. But then the winner emails you and says that he or she will send you a cashier's check for the $10,000 dollars and ask you to wire him funds for the difference between the cashier's check and the value of the car.

The natural inclination at this point is to go along because you want the deal to go through, and a cashier's check is always good right? Wrong! Cashier's checks are often forged, but it can take banks weeks to discover that the check was forged. When it does, you will be out the $4000, plus possibly the car as well.

Sometimes online thieves are focused more on stealing you identity than your cash. These are sophisticated cybercriminals who will harvest social security numbers and others bits of identity and then pass them on to others who will steal your identity to commit all kinds of frauds from credit cards to equity lines to car rentals and hotel stays.

This particular fraud is known as *phishing*, because it works just like a worm on a pole in the water—only you're the big one they're waiting to land. Any number of large companies has been a victim of this from banking companies to computer auction companies, but the way the scam works is pretty much the same. You'll get an email from an eBay look-a-like site. The email will be very good. It will in fact almost completely mimic an email from eBay. It will say something like due to increased security measures we are asking you to reconfirm your personal identification info. Then it will have screens to fill out where you can put in your name, social security number, address, and perhaps mothers maiden name since many banks use that as a tag identifier. Then thinking everything is perfectly safe, you'll email it back to them. But, it was all a scam. The email never really came from eBay or Citicorp or whomever. It came from a cyberciminal who was hoping to ensnare innocent people into giving up personal information so they could steal their identities.

Another path to ruin for many online users starts when they leave, say eBay, and go offline to do a separate deal. Say you are selling an item on eBay for a fairly substantial amount of money, but you didn't get any bids. Or you didn't get the reserve amount you wanted, so you decided not to sell the object. Once the auction is done you get an email from a buyer suggesting you go offline to finish the transaction or just sell it directly to them. Don't do it! eBay, as well as most online auction sites, offers buyers and sellers certain protections that do not apply if the deal is done off site. There are some steps you should take as a seller. One of these is that you should actually read all the information eBay and the others put up about security. But you should *read the rules for each site.* Yahoo differs from Amazon and from eBay and so forth.

There are major and minor points to be aware of as an online seller. First just as in brick and mortar sales, try to determine how much your object is worth before you try to sell it. After you have a rough idea, set a number for the minimum bid you'll accept. Then weigh the benefits and costs of setting a minimum or reserve price or set the opening bid high enough to protect yourself.

The second point is a more minor point but as the seller, always make sure you check the box that shows that the buyer is to pay for the shipping costs. Also spell out in the listing that the buyer pays for premium shipping if he or she wants it. As a seller, it's really in your interest to ship through some kind of service like U.S. priority mail or UPS that has a tracking number system. That way you'll know at least the package was delivered to the buyer's door if there's ever problem. Also, as a seller, think about refund policies. They are a huge pain, but they may increase sales.

As a seller you should be suspicious if the buyer wants to use an *escrow service* but will only use one particular company. An escrow is not necessarily an online concept. Escrows have been used by many years in real estate transaction in particular. An escrow is a third party that holds the funds and only releases them when the conditions of the deal are met. However, a fraudulent escrow holder never releases the fund, they just take them. So the seller is out the merchandise and the money. Further, if you agree to use the service, you may be asked to set up an account with them that requires you to disclose personal information such as you social security number, birth date, or mother's maiden name. Then, the escrow service and buyer can steal your identity with the data you've supplied them for the fake account.

Another thing to consider is that you have to be honest when you sell items online. For example, when you advertise things for sale, you must to accurately describe them. This means the usual things you would suspect, such as price, volume, quantity, and quality. This is because under federal law, you are required to advertise your product honestly and accurately. Also, just as it would be wrong for you to have people in the audience at a physical auction place fake bids, it's wrong for you to have your buddies act as *shills* on your electronic auction as well. A shill is someone planted in the audience at an auction who doesn't really want the item but bids on it anyway to run up the price.

There is another federal law of which Internet auction sellers also need to be aware. As a seller of goods under the Federal Trade Commission's *Mail or Telephone Order Merchandise Rule,* you must be able to send your goods out within a specified time. This means when the auction ends or with thirty days you have to be able to send the buyer his or her stuff, give them back their money, or give them the opportunity to ask for a refund.

BRICK AND MORTAR AUCTIONS

If you only have one item to sell or you hate computers, you may be able to take your item to an auction. To take your item to the auctions like they have on the PBS *At the Auction*, you have to have a valuable item. But local houses may be more willing to take items in to sell. Like antique dealers, auction houses are in the business of having auctions and to have auction, they have to have inventory. You should be prepared though to call several of them. If you were getting rid of a whole household of stuff, then they might be willing to come to you. But for small items or only one item, you will probably have to take it to them. Definitely call before going since they may not accept items like yours. If they do, then they will charge you a percentage of what the item brings.

Naturally, you don't get paid until the items sells and the auctioneer gets paid. But when they do, they deduct their auctioneer's commission for selling the item. The commission amount comes from the last bid that becomes the final *hammer price* when the auctioneer announces it to the crowd and then either says the item has closed or bangs his or her gavel.

ADS

You may be able to put your item in the free want *ads* and sell it easily. Before eBay or the *Internet Antique Store* existed, plenty of items were sold this way and plenty still do. Obviously, the trick is to put your ad in where you will get the most mileage at the lowest cost. Think of the local free shopper papers rather than slick metropolitan dailies. If you're goal is to raise cash, you don't want to tie up money in this project.

Successful ads that sell items have all of the essentials such as your phone number, a brief description of the item, and how much you are asking for it. There are good and bad points to setting a price. It may discourage some people, but you really only want to hear from serious callers who are prepared to pay a reasonable price for your item. The other thing you will need with an ad is either someone to answer the phone 24-7 or an answering machine. If you have an answering machine, make sure it sounds like one that people will be willing to talk to.

Finally, you have to plan how to show off your item to perspective buyers. There are some basic things you need to do. First look at it as if you were seeing it for the first time and looking to buy it yourself. If it can be cleaned safely without harming its value, clean it. (See Dangers of Cleaning up Antiques and Collectibles p.103.) Then take a hint from every retail store you've ever been in. Set the piece up in the room so it looks like a winner. Also, make sure the piece is ready to go when the buyer pays for it. That means you have all of your stuff out of it before you even show it.

GARAGE SALES

Depending on the weather and your personality, a garage sales could be the most fun you've ever had raising cash quick—or absolute misery. Before you even contemplate this option, ask yourself, am I willing to do deal with the general public? Can I set a firm price? Can I tell someone they cannot use my bathroom or go inside my house, but that the gas station at the end of the block has a public bathroom? If the answer is yes, you could be off to the races. However, there are many other options available to raising quick cash that are less work and far less aggravation.

There are certain steps that must be taken to ensure that your garage sale succeeds. First and most important is timing. Some things like the weather cannot be cured and must be endured. Keep your eyes wide open for any evidence of garage sales. Call the city. See when the block closings are for garage sales before you schedule yours. More than any other factor, your garage sale depends on enough foot traffic to attract sufficient lookers that you can turn into buyers.

Second, think big and plan early. Can you do a block wide garage sale? Some shoppers might not come over for one, but who could resist ten at once. This option only works if you have the time though.

Assuming you are only interested in doing a sale for your family, then you need to keep the costs as low as possible and increase the profits by getting as much stuff as possible out to attract buyers. Some specific hints for this are having a wide variety of items for adults and children. Lighting is very important as well. The inventory needs to be as well lit as possible.

Another helpful hint is to make your prices end with quarters so you don't need to make change. When pricing items, you want to make it as simple as possible. Cruise a couple garage sales to get a reasonable estimate, then price everything solidly in the middle.

One of the key developments you need to consider very seriously is security for your profits as well as yourself. Garage sales that really hit, can generate hundreds of dollars if not thousands. Think about what you are going to do with the money. Take a hint from farmers market vendors—avoid cash boxes because it's just too easy for someone to come up, reach in, and steal it. Instead wear an apron and keep the cash on your person where it's harder to steal.

Secondly, many businesses make sure they never have too much cash on hand by making several cash drops throughout the day. Have a partner available who can run the money to where you are stashing it periodically. It's not a good idea to run any sale by yourself, if you can help it. Two are usually safer than one. So be sure to get a partner.

There are many books available to help in planning a garage sale including *Have a Garage Sale and Make Some Money* by Sally Rofe and *Garage Sale Magic!: How to Turn Your 'Trash' into Cash* by Pam Williams. There are also quite a few checklists for garage sales on the Web, including:

www.hgtv.com/hgtv/pac_ctnt_lnb_gutter/text
/0,1783,HGTV_3938_12265,FF.html

STOCKS & OTHER SECURITIES

This seems straight forward. If the stock is not held in an investment vehicle such as a 401(k) it should be quick and easy. Borrowing against stock is discussed in Chapter 4, but there's nothing that says the stock cannot be sold directly to generate quick cash. You just need to have the shares themselves or know which broker you are using that is holding the actual shares. Then all you have to do is call the sale order in and in a few days you will have the money.

However there are some potential downsides to directly selling stock to raise cash quickly. First of all, the market may be terrible. You may have had the bad luck to be selling when everything is down. But either way, once you've sold, you're done. On the other hand, if the stock had been doing badly and there were no reasonable hopes for an upturn, this would be a great time to sell.

Secondly, whenever you sell stock, you have the potential for paying tax on the proceeds. If you've only had the stock for a short time, then you have to pay on the gains as *ordinary income*. If you have owned the stock for a long enough period, then you can claim the gains as a *long-term capital gain* at a much lower rate. If you are contemplating selling a large value portfolio when you only need to raise a small amount of cash you should definitely consider borrowing against the value of your portfolio instead.

The above advice also assumes that the stock you plan on selling is a stock that is freely traded on a public exchange like the New York Stock Exchange. If you have stock in a small company that is not traded and you want to sell it to raise cash quick, it may be harder to do. Often small closely-held companies have intricate buy-sell agreements that control how the stock is to be sold and who may buy it. If you do have this kind of stock, check to see if there are buy-sell agreements governing the sale of the stock. It's also unlikely that people will be willing to lend you money on this stock as collateral since they will have the same problems involved in selling it.

TRADITIONAL AND ROTH IRA ACCOUNTS

An *individual retirement account* or *IRA* is a way that people save for their retirement. It allows the person to build resources through tax deferral. Because the program comes with many tax benefits, it also has several requirements that must be met for an early withdrawal (like all tax deferred investments).

There are traditional and Roth IRAs. Both have complex requirements for taking money out early. However they can be significant sources of cash, and the Roth may be a good choice for meeting some unexpected expenses.

To sell you account is a two-step process. First, the form has to be filed with the institution that has custody of the account. This information can be located on your account statement, a Web page, or phone directory. Once the paperwork is completed, it should take about a week or so for internal processing. You should expect some resistance from your bank or other custodian. Some is self-interest and some is not.

EXAMPLE: Banks may steer you away from cashing in your IRA because of the potential taxes that you will have to pay. Unless you fit into one of the exemptions, you will have to pay a 10% penalty.

However, banks are in the business of making loans, so their natural instinct will be to steer you toward a refinancing, mortgage, or other type of home equity loan. Only listen to them if you have a job or other very stable source of income from self-employment. (Generally speaking, if you need money because you are unemployed or laid off you are probably wasting your time trying to get a loan from a bank.)

After you have sent the form in, you may have to deal with the tax issues. The IRS wants people to pay money into their IRAs and leave it there. So there is a 10% penalty on early withdrawals or distributions made before age 59½.

However, there are several exceptions that you may fit under. If you fit under one of the exceptions, then you could take the money out without paying the 10% penalty tax. For example, you can roll over to another IRA or qualified retirement plan and not be subject to this 10% additional tax. Also, if the owner dies and distributes the money to a beneficiary or estate, it is a tax-free transfer. Another idea, if you find you need cash quickly because of a medical condition, is the disability exception. (However, think serious disability, not something that will be cured relatively quickly.)

If the distributions are made as part of a series of substantially equal, periodic payments over your life or life expectancy, then you can avoid the tax. This option requires serious research and you may want to run it by a lawyer or tax professional. An easier and perhaps more useful exception might be the qualified first–time home purchase. Also of interest to the returning college student would be the qualified higher education expense option.

But the most useful fact of IRA distributions is that that penalty-free distributions can be made for payment of medical insurance premiums that the person needs to pay while he or she is unemployed. Distributions can also be made for unreimbursed medical expenses that are more than 7.5% of your adjusted gross income.

Refer to the IRS publications for guidance on how to fill out your tax returns, as well as how to pay if you do not fall under an exception.

529 AND COVERDELL (EDUCATIONAL) IRA ACCOUNTS

A 529 College Plan is named after the part of the tax code that created it. It is a college savings plan run by state governments that allows individuals to easily and readily begin to put money away for college expenses for their children and grandchildren. Money can be taken out of the college plan as an early withdrawal. The money for college would be available when the child is ready to go to school. But if parents needed the money back before that time, then money could be taken out.

The application and information from the plan administrator should have a phone number. If there's a website for the plan, it may have information on how to make an early withdrawal. This will depend on the individual state plan and its requirements and administrators.

The biggest advantages are that this plan allows people to get what would be their own money back. It also avoids the high cost of borrowing money and the credit check and all that goes with it.

Some states require you to give up any investment gain, others require a percentage of the plan be paid as a penalty. In addition, be sure to see what state tax implications will be triggered by an early withdrawal. The federal rules are that you must pay a 10% penalty and that you pay tax on the income at your usual rate. Specific states may require you to pay more in penalties as well.

An educational IRA or Coverdell account is a savings vehicle for accumulating money for a college education for a child. Its main advantage is that money deposited into it grows tax free. Money can be taken out of the account, but it is subject to fairly narrow exceptions. For example, if early withdrawals are made and the money is not used for education, there may be both a 10% penalty and the responsibility of paying taxes on the money. Like the IRA, the government goal is for the money to grow tax free. Once it comes out, then the government will consider it taxable.

INTERNAL ASSETS

Blood, plasma, semen, and eggs are literally the stuff of life, and there is a good market for three out of four of the items. There is enormous variance in how much you can get paid and for what liquid asset you have to sell. Blood is not a good candidate for sale. Plasma, however, is a good possibility. Semen is too, and eggs could be quite a good one depending on several factors.

Blood and Plasma

Blood sales have been discouraged greatly since the advent of HIV and AIDS. There were fears that the rates of HIV and AIDS were higher in blood from people who were paid to give blood than from people who volunteered. So blood is not a good option for raising cash anymore. The Red Cross even has a policy against paying donors cash or cash equivalents.

Plasma, on the other hand, presents an area of opportunity for those who are healthy and have no fear of needles or medical procedures. Estimates range as high as $600 a month for plasma sales. The amount of money that can be raised depends on how often the person is willing to donate and the quality of their plasma. Individuals who have been vaccinated against hepatitis B may be able to command a premium for their plasma. Plasma and blood centers can be located in the paper, yellow pages, or online by searching for *blood* or *plasma*.

However, anyone contemplating using this strategy is cautioned to consider it seriously. While this procedure is not as invasive as donating eggs, it is considerably more involved than donating blood. This is because not only does the person's blood have to be extracted and the plasma separated out, but also then it has to be reinfused into the donor. This process often goes well, but it may not go well all the time for everyone. A lot of how the process goes seems to depend on the skill of the person inserting the various needles into the donor.

Some of the precautions are ones that would apply to donating blood. Donors should eat beforehand and drink plenty of fluids to replace those that are lost. People with small veins are not good donors. In addition, the plasma centers will have requirements as to minimum weight.

Sperm

It may be possible for you to raise cash by donating sperm. Fertility centers and clinics are the big purchasers. To become a sperm donor, the fertility clinic has to ask you questions about your lifestyle and genetic history. Sexual diseases are a big no-no and so are bad genetics. You can expect to have to take a physical, undergo medical testing, and to donate a sample for testing.

Think under a $100 per donation. However, generally, if your profile of health and genetics make you a good candidate, then fertility clinics may wish to have you donate several times. The law is well settled that sperm donors do not have parental rights to children produced by their sperm if it is done according to the requirements of the state statutes that govern it. (Family law is generally a matter of state law and not federal law in the United States.)

It may not, however, be a source of quick cash if you need the cash within a week or so. All the testing and evaluation can take months. Then you have got to make the actual donations. Think in terms of a couple donations a week. Then after six months, you have will follow-up visits. Fertility clinics want to make absolutely certain they are not passing on sperm from a man with a sexually transmitted disease.

Eggs

Of these options, eggs are by far the most potentially lucrative methods of raising cash. However, this is not an option for the faint hearted. Paying donors for their eggs is a very controversial process. Though it is legal, anyone contemplating doing it should check at the time of the procedure. The fees can by quite large ranging into the thousands of dollars in come cases. However, just as this is the most highly compensated of the body items you might sell, it is the most inconvenient by far.

Harvesting eggs out of a woman's body is, by its very nature, an invasive surgical procedure. Additionally, unless hormones are used, women will only have one egg per month to donate. So to make the procedure effective, it's necessary to titillate the ovaries so they produce as much as they can. Then there is another injection to release the eggs. Finally, they extract them through the surgical procedure. Timing is crucial and the health risks are certainly something to be weighed carefully.

The egg donor is also going to have to undergo psychological assessment to see if she's a good candidate for coping with the issues involved in having a part of her become someone else's child. A donor gives up all of her parental rights to a child that comes from her eggs.

If you plan to donate sperm, you probably don't need to contact a lawyer first. But, if you are planning to donate your eggs and receive compensation for them, you should definitely consider seeking the advice of a lawyer in your state who is familiar with the issues involved. Do not be shy about asking if he or she has done one of these contracts before.

Earn It

6

Earning money is pretty straightforward. You perform a job and get paid for it. At one time, perhaps that would be all the options there were, but not now. Options for earning money abound and range from traditional employer-employee relations to Internet freelancing where people never physically meet. Almost any ability or service can potentially be used to raise cash. This chapter explores several options such as full-time work, part-time work, freelancing, and independent business possibilities. There is also a section on some opportunities to be wary of.

All of these activities are regulated to some extent by federal and state law. For example, federal law and policy determines minimum wage levels, minimum job safety standards, taxes, and social security. Working as an independent contractor has its own regulatory challenges since it entails taking over many of the responsibilities handled by an employer.

TEMPORARY WORK

Temporary workers or *temps* are employees of one company who work for a different company on a short-term basis. Temping is one of the fastest growing segments in the whole U.S. economy. In fact, some observers of the U.S. labor market estimate that the largest employer in the U.S. is *Manpower Temporary Services.*

The traditional temping idea is that it is an option for a secretary who was temporarily between jobs or just wanted some part-time work while the kids were at school. This is a severely out of date idea. The reality of today's job market is that temps come in all sizes, shapes, and backgrounds ranging from temporary receptionists to engineers and executives.

The process actually begins with a company that has a need for workers, but need works done more than it needs an employee. Hiring a full-time employee is an expensive time-consuming, risky proposition for an employer. Sometimes it is worth paying a premium for the labor to get someone else to do the hiring, record keeping, firing, and the complying with all the federal and state laws that go with having an employee. Plus, the need may be very short. Why get a full-time employee that will have to be fired after a two-week job when a temp can be brought in quickly and easily? Although assignments can be as short as a day, they can also be as long as years.

After the agency gets the order from an employer, the agency negotiates a price with that employer. The spread between what the employer pays the temporary agency and what the temporary agency pays the temp is where the agency makes its money. The agency gets to keep the difference between what the company is willing to pay it for administering and recruiting the workers and what the workers are willing to take to do the work. Of course, all of this is still subject to applicable federal and state labor laws, including minimum wage and workers' compensation.

For the person who needs to raise cash, getting a temp job is a lot like getting any other job. The temping firm becomes the employer of the person—just like any other job. In fact, temps who work long enough at a temping agency can get vacation and health insurance benefits. However, as a practical matter, these often take many hours of temp assignments to qualify for. The other disadvantage can be that the health insurance may not be very good and it may cost a lot relative to the benefits that you receive.

The actual job application will proceed like many others. You send in a resume. It is matched up against potential openings. Then you go in for an interview. One big difference is that many (though not all, by any means) temp jobs require office skills such as typing and filing. So you will probably have to take skills tests for typing and other abilities.

Temping firms are listed in the print and electronic Yellow Pages. Many job sites on the web also list temping firms, as well as traditional job-hunting sources, such as the Sunday want ads. Even though it is a temporary placement, it is still a job. This means you should think in terms of weeks, not days. If you have a skill that is particularly in demand, then you might figure a very short wait of a few days to receive your first assignment.

Temping is based on the business swings in the economy as a whole. Temps are generally the first people hired when things improve and business picks up. They are definitely the first people fired when the business cycle slows down or businesses need to save money.

Temping offers many advantages to the person just seeking cash, as well as to the full-time job seeker. Survey after survey shows that most temp workers would prefer full-time jobs. And yet some are just moonlighting or picking up cash after their regular jobs or during summer vacations from school.

Temping's biggest advantage is that it's about the easiest way to get something approximating a full-time job. The other advantage is that if you are looking for a job, it lets you try the job, the boss, and the company on for size before accepting a full-time position. In a month you could work at four different jobs in four different companies. This lets you audition whole industries for a job, as well as meeting people you would never meet in your normal routine. The pay, depending on what you are doing, can be pretty good. Expect a low of minimum wage on up to hundreds of dollars an hour for professionals with skills in demand.

One of the touted advantages of temping is that the person can work when he or she wants to. If you have hot skills and the market is good, this could indeed be true. However, if you are doing it because you need or really want the money, you'll want to be working whenever you can. It's possible to turn down assignments, but that's not a good way to win points with the agency. Temping agencies only make money when they have people working.

Disadvantages

The pay you receive for temping often lags behind that of regular employees by a significant margin. It is quite possible to be working side by side a full-time employee doing the exact same job for half of the money and none of the benefits.

The number one thing temps complain about next to the low pay is being treated like a potted plant. Actually in some cases, the potted plants may actually be treated with more respect than the temporary workers. In other offices, temps make life long friends and networking contacts.

Another potentially huge disadvantage to this type of job is that the temp employee has absolutely no idea of what kind of situation he or she is getting into. For example, it pays to ask lots of questions and then ask even more. A big concern can be work place safety issues, ranging from exposure to dangerous chemicals to bad neighborhoods and physical assaults.

Back in the days of more stable employment, people who had temped often feared it would look as if they were not good, long-term employees. However, some experts have suggested that the average job can only be expected to last for a few years. So a period of temping will not necessarily look out of place on a resume.

Another disadvantage is that time spent on temp assignments is time that cannot be spent on full-time job searchers. This also serves to underscore another point that time spent with temping agencies also may not lend itself to maxing out the 401(k) or generating time spent to qualify for pensions. Temping is usually strictly a cash-and-carry sort of business.

The temping arrangement is very much an employer-employee relationship. As such, the same kind of regulations and rules will be present that most employees will already be aware of. Employees are paid wages that the employer (temping agency) must deduct applicable federal and state taxes from. In addition, state workers compensation laws and unemployment compensation laws also apply. Although any worker filing for unemployment insurance compensation may be in for a rough application process since temping agencies often do not want to pay unemployment claims.

This is a very cyclical business. The greatest irony is that just when you've been laid off or unemployed because the economy is in the dumps is the time that companies are most likely to cut back on their temp needs. In fact, one of the benefits that companies derive from temping is that they can reduce their payrolls without paying out severance or unemployment claims.

FREELANCING

Freelancing is such an ancient practice in human history that the term supposedly comes down to us from the middle ages. A knight who lost or fell out of favor from his superior would be said to now be a free lancer. This meant that he belonged to no superior and he was a free agent. The term is used in a similar manner today.

Throughout history, small business people have often hired each other during peak times for money or reciprocal labor agreements. Before huge firms, lawyers often asked other lawyers to work with them on cases. Farmers in particular have often swapped labor or cash in helping each other out with various farm jobs. So, it's definitely not a new concept. It's more of a very old concept that went underground during the time of stable 9-5 job arrangements.

A freelancer or *independent contractor* is someone who is hired to do a specific job and when the job is through, the person is done working for the company or employer. This means that the person has no obligation to the company. It also means that the company has no obligation to the person.

Some services lend themselves particularly well to freelancing. Writing is an industry filled with freelancing. All you need to be able to write is have the ability and motivation and a typewriter or computer. The start-up costs is fairly low compared to other possibilities.

The process of obtaining a freelancing position can be quite simple. Using writing as an example, a writer asks an editor of a magazine if they are interested in a story on a certain topic. If the editor is interested and the person fits the bill of whom they had in mind to write the story, then the author gives them the story. There may or may not be a formal contract. (Generally speaking though, there should always be a formal contract that spells out how much work, sets standards for the quality of the work, and identifies the rate of pay for the work.)

Believe it or not, if you've just been downsized, your former employer may be the best hirer of you for freelancing. Think about it, you know the people, the place, the industry, and the requirements. Just because companies do not want employees does not mean they don't want work done.

As a rule of thumb, it's much easier to do the same job you were doing for someone else. As an example, if you were an assembly line worker putting on bolts for Ford, it's not a major change to go to GM and say, "I'd like to put on bolts for you." However, if you want to switch jobs within the same industry, that's a bit harder. The hardest transition of all is to change jobs and change industries at the sometime. For example, if you were a shepherd and decided to become a car salesman, that would be quite a switch. And although it might be easier to pick up a freelancing or moonlighting job doing it, it still would not be the easiest thing to do.

After you have considered your former employer, think of other companies within the industry where you could apply the same skills. After that, consider industries that are similar to the one you just left.

Freelancing has more in common with temping than it does being an employee. If a company and a person have the need and the money, then they will be looking quite hard. If they don't, then they won't. It is a given that you have to be able to convince them that you can do the job, but after meeting those barriers the next challenge is to find them at the right time. Freelancing very much depends on the market as a whole.

You should also know that as a freelancer you are more like a small business than an employee. You can take deductions on your taxes that employees could never deduct. However, unlike being an employee, you now need to keep very accurate records of how much you make and how much you spend.

Also, if you plan on providing these services under a name different from your own, then you should explore whether you need to register a *doing business as certificate* with the local authorities, such as the county or state where the business will be operated. If you are a sole proprietorship; your name is Susan Adams; and, you operate as Susan Adams Bakeshop, it is clear who the legal owner is. If, however, you are Susan Adams and you operate as The Eureka Bakery, you will need to register and get a *doing business as certificate* to show that you are operating as The Eureka Bakery.

If you plan on doing the freelancing from your home, you should also know what the rules are for businesses—specifically home-based businesses in your locale. Assume for just a second that you do consulting from your home and it takes off and goes really well. Do you really want to have to move to an office because of zoning? A little research at the start may be a lot less costly than a big change later on.

You should definitely approach freelancing from the very beginning as a self-employed person providing a business service. This means thinking of things in a far different way than you would have as an employee. As an employee, even if marketing is your job, it is the company's product that you are marketing. As a freelancer, you are the company, product, and marketing manager all rolled into one.

There are a host of resources you should be aware of. Freelancing and independent contracting arrangements flourished in the days of the dot.com. So not surprisingly, many of the resources are on the Internet.

Advantages and Disadvantages

Like every other way of raising cash it has advantages and disadvantages. The greatest advantage is that it's fast and easy—assuming you can do the job. Another huge advantage is that freelancing may allow you to only do the parts of your job that you are good at or that you like. For example, let's say you are a manager charged with project management responsibility over all aspects of the projects. You may love the planning stages of project management. But, perhaps personnel issues drive you to the point of madness and you just can't stand them. Freelancing may allow you to work with companies during the planning stage exclusively. By the time the fights and the firings happen, instead of refereeing them, you'll be long gone and on to another consulting job.

Another aspect that may make you feel freelancing is not for you is that you have to be able to negotiate rates with customers and clients. As an employee, you may only have to talk dollars and cents once a year when you have an annual review. As a freelancer, you have to be prepared to negotiate your own deal each time. As an employee, you'll have the consolation of knowing most everybody at your level is making about what you are. As a freelancer, you have to eat your own cooking. If you underbid the job you'll be stuck with two miserable choices—keep working for peanuts or back out and risk getting any repeat business with the customer again.

Another aspect of freelancing that is very much like having a small business is that you will always be looking for the next project. If you love marketing, this is a dream position. If you hate it, you will soon wind up with no more assignments or projects.

Two other aspects of small business come into play as a freelancer. First the IRS has very specific requirements that you must meet for you to be considered an independent contractor. For more details see their website at **www.irs.gov** and their Publication 1779 independent contractor or employee.

There are several different factors that go into deciding if a person is an independent contractor or employee. But one of the crucial factors is who controls how the work is done. A true independent contractor arrangement is like when you hire a plumber. You tell the plumber what you want done, but you don't supervise the work and instruct how you want it done. The essential element with this test is to have a *written contract* that spells out the work that is to be done and the amount of money that will be paid to the contractor upon successful completion of the job.

Successfully working as an independent contractor means mastering a new series of tax obligations. As an employee, much of the income tax work is done by the employer. As an independent contractor, the responsibility is that of the worker. Employees get their income on a W-2 that gets attached to their tax return. Independent contractors must file a Schedule C with their tax return, which shows their net income from their business activities. As an independent contractor, you'll need to add up all the payments you received and subtract from them all of the authorized deductions. In addition to this requirement, as a self-employed individual you will be responsible for estimating your income and filing the appropriate tax payments throughout the year. Last, but certainly not least, as an employee the employer matches half of the Social Security tax obligation, but as a self-employed individual, you must pay the whole tax.

There are other considerations you should definitely be aware of if you choose to freelance. These can include such items as insurance, taxes, and who owns what you create for the person doing the project. There is a crucial distinction between employees and freelancers or independent contractors. Employees have their income taxes withheld by their employer. Independent contractors have to pay their own. The government goes through a multifactored analysis to figure out which status workers fit into.

If you are being paid as an independent contractor on a form 1099, you will have to do you own withholding. As far as the insurance goes, you are on your own. If you hurt someone you may be liable under your own insurance. And finally as an employee generally speaking ideas you create on company time and equipment belong to the employer. If you are doing the project completely on your own with your own equipment, then it belongs to you. If someone else has hired you to do it, then the ownership becomes blurred.

As such, you may have to sign a *work for hire* agreement. This means that what you create belongs to the person who hired you to do it. If for example you are hired to do a painting to commemorate some hugely important day in the history of the company and that was your regular job, the rights to the painting would belong to the company as your employer. If however they hired you as a freelancer and said paint a picture, without a written agreement giving them the right to the picture, it could well belong to you.

The alternative to addressing this question with a contract may be to have the IRS make the determination. The IRS has a procedure where the independent contractor and the employee can submit a form SS-8 that is available on the IRS website at **www.irs.gov**. The form asks questions in four areas: behavioral control, financial control, relationship of the worker and the firm, and a special section for salespersons. Questions are asked regarding how the worker will be paid, whether the individual has other clients and advertises, and specific questions related to sales such as who supplies the leads and what products exactly does the salesperson sell.

Specific Websites

Freelancers can post their availability for assignments on many different websites. These websites allow companies and individuals who need services the chance to find people who can do the work for them. Many websites serve the specific industry of their members. Others focus on the whole gamut of potential services. For example, there are many newsletters and websites for authors who are looking for assignments such as **www.worldwidefreelance.com**, **www.writersdigest.com**, and **http://freelancewrite.about.com**. There are also websites available for the high tech market such as **www.skillserve.com**.

Elance, at **www.elance.com**, is an example of a web-based service that providers can subscribe to for a fee. It allows the person who wants to do the freelancing the chance to post a description of what they can do on a website that companies or persons who wants to purchase the service can then take a look at. While there are several advantages to elance, it's not particularly cheap. Basic registration is $70 a month, but it can get your proposal out in front of a lot of people. Before getting started, you should take a look at the background information in the FAQ sections on the site. It is a good intro to the site and an excellent overview of the whole world of freelancing.

Another site that has free basic registration is **www.bizmoonlighter.com**. It is the successor to **www.guru.com**. This is a site well worth looking at if you are interested in doing freelance work.

Business Planning

Freelancing requires planning and budgeting. You do not have to produce a thirty year strategy for dominating your market niche, but you owe it to yourself to do a little bit of business and life planning. The freelancing that you're doing right now for a temporary financial crisis may wind itself up naturally at the end of the temporary crisis that caused you to need the cash or it may be the beginning of a major phase of your professional life. Either way, spend some time planning before doing.

There are many opportunities and problems with going out on your own. One of the biggest is that instead of being an employee hired to do the work, now you are a small business owner responsible for *doing* the work as well as *getting* the work.

To do the minimum amount of planning, you should, as a freelancer, consider the essential points of the service you intend to provide and about yourself. William Bridges has written a great book for anyone contemplating being a freelancer: *Creating You & Co Learning To Think Like The CEO Of Your Own Career.* In a nutshell ask yourself the following questions.

- ◆ What services can I provide that people will pay for?
- ◆ Who can I provide services to?
- ◆ How will I market my services?
- ◆ How much will I charge?
- ◆ Where do I want to do this?
- ◆ How much income do I need?

◆ How many hours of work does this translate into per week, per month, and per year?

By the time you finish thinking through these questions, you should be able to talk and think about the opportunity that actually presents itself. The questions are designed so that when you have answered them, you have a rough plan for going forward. Any plan needs to address the money, the marketing, and making it happen.

Small Business Administration

A business plan can be enormously complicated or it can be written on the back of an index card. It is not whether the finished product is perfect. It is the planning that goes into it. One of the best resources is at the federal Small Business Association website:

www.sba.gov/starting_business/planning/writingplan.html

The SBA site also has links to sample business plans that can help you in thinking through all the issues. For the kinds of businesses that you might be interested in starting to generate quick cash, the most important thing is that your plan must have a complete and detailed explanation of costs. The goal is a business that can get going on a shoestring and that will not wind up costing you money.

An example of a simple business plan to start a dog walking service may look like the following.

Goal: To start a dog walking service that will bring in $100 a week.

Market: My friends and neighbors.

Budget: List all the costs such as insurance bonding, leasing, and business permits

Strengths: I love dogs and worked in a vet clinic.

Weaknesses: I hate math and don't like asking people for money.

Opportunities: I have six neighbors and friends that I can charge $10 a day.

Threats: Five other people in the neighborhood do this.

Marketing: I will post my services with a phone number in every grocery store in a six-block neighborhood.

An essential resource that can greatly help with this process is your local *Small Business Development Center* or SBDC. Their website is located at **http://sbdcnet.utsa.edu**. It has links to an impressive collection of small business information including a very helpful section on home businesses. The site also includes a state-by-state guide to locating a Small Business Development Center in your area.

PART-TIME JOBS AND OVERTIME

The easiest source of quick cash may be a *part-time job* or *overtime* from your existing job. If you are paid by the hour and your employer has overtime, that's probably the easiest way to raise cash around.

Advantages and Disadvantages

The advantages are huge. You don't have to go into debt or sell personal items you may be attached to. Your employer may even regard you as a great team player who's willing to go the extra mile.

The disadvantages are that it takes more time and more energy. Also, if you have child-care arrangement in place, think carefully of what you will do if you choose to work overtime. If you have bad luck with child care, it might easily wind up eating up all the cash you made from the overtime. Also, factor in whether overtime will deliver the cash you need fast enough. Even though overtime has many advantages it also has one big drawback, it can take time, and lots of it, to generate cash.

Part-time work may also be a relatively quick and easy way to raise some cash. Many people have two and three jobs successfully at the same time. In fact, one of the ways to break into a new industry is to do part-time work. This allows you to not only bring in cash, but also acquire benefits as well.

Best Employers

Finding the best part-time employer for your needs depends a lot on you and your very own unique reasons for wanting to raise cash. However, acquiring a part-time job is like any other money making endeavor, think net, not gross—how much you make on a job minus all the expenses, financial and emotional, to make that money.

For example, if one part-time job is thirty miles away but pays more than one you can walk to, balance out the rates of pay. You want to raise as much as you can in the shortest period of time. Anything that costs you money, such as transportation, depreciation on a car, or meals you have to buy away from home is definitely a consideration.

Unless you're asking your present employer for more work through overtime or additional hours, a work opportunity should get the same analysis that any other option would receive under the cash flow analysis in Chapter 2. Since the end result is to raise cash quickly, the best employer is the one that will allow you to raise the most cash quickly with the lowest amount of expense. Always think end result.

Worst Employers

Usually a bad employer leaves clues. If you fill out the application or go to the interview and something doesn't seem right, then leave and don't go back. Keep looking. A bad employment choice in a quest for quick cash is almost worse than no employment. A bad choice will take three things that must be managed carefully during a hunt for quick cash: time, energy, and focus.

That does not mean that you should in any part abandon your hunt for employment. If after looking at the options, a job full-time or part-time seems like the best way to raise cash, then any and all options should be followed through on. Just avoid any employer that will wind up costing you money, time, and aggravation.

Networking

The absolute best way to get a part-time job is to network through someone you know. This way you have an in who can let you know what the real deal is. A buddy or relative who works at the place can let you know who the good supervisor is and who the horrible one is. He or she can let you know where to park cheap or which train to take. Many smaller companies may in fact only list part-time opportunities through insiders.

Assuming you are lacking in the insider arrangement, the next easiest way to find a part-time job is by just looking around when you're out and about. The number one way most new customers come into a business is that they were going by and saw the sign. Companies with real part-time jobs are not shy. The put up signs in the window or they advertise.

Another good source of part-time jobs is the local paper or the local shopper paper. Generally speaking, ads in the local paper and the free shopper papers are much cheaper than ads in the major daily papers. This means local employers may be more willing to advertise in these papers. Employers who will be advertising in these papers are also very likely to be advertising real jobs instead of just shopping the market to see what talent is available.

The job process for part-time jobs is usually less formal than a full-time job. You can expect to fill out an application and go through an interview. The job application process can take any place from weeks to days to being hire on the spot. Part-time jobs often are subject to many of the same rules as full-time employees. However, the biggest one is that generally part-time employees are not eligible for group medical benefits.

ODD JOBS AND JOBS THAT ARE ODD

Necessity may be the mother of invention. It certainly can be the parent of unique jobs. The jobs in this section are connected by one common theme: people who want to raise cash quickly may find them to be a means to that end. This section discusses being a human guinea pig for profit, doing mystery shopping, and joining a product focus group.

Medical Subject

If you live near a large university, you may be able to get a paid assignment as a medical subject. Psych labs used to be big consumers of people for use in human studies. Researchers using human subjects are highly supervised and regulated, so you should be safe. It's not always available and it won't pay that great—but it could be an option. You will also have to fit the profile exactly of the subjects the researchers are looking for.

The website of *Guinea Pigs Get Paid* at **www.gpgp.net/faq.htm** is definitely a resource well worth looking at. It also might be worth a trip to the *So You Wanna* website at **www.soyouwanna.com/site/syws/ guineapig/guineapig3.html**. This website says it will teach you the things you didn't learn in school. It has very good resources on being a human subject.

There are several legal and regulatory issues involved in this strategy. First you will have to sign an informed consent form that details the procedure and acknowledges that you've been informed of the risk.

Second, the money you receive will be taxable income for you. The research institution will report to the IRS that it paid you the money for being a test subject.

Focus Group Member

Some people make a small, but significant part-time income doing *focus groups* for marketing companies. To find out about whether this is an opportunity, ask around and find someone who's doing it. It's generally not a competitive process since the companies seeking the consumer input generally have very specific requirements for participants. Either you fit the profile or you don't. If you can't find a person you know who is doing this already, you can check the Yellow Pages online or in print for marketing research and analysis firms. Generally, doing the survey either involves just answering questions or it may involve sampling products and giving back feedback.

This can be a fairly quick and pleasant way to bring in some cash. Think hundreds, not thousands of hours of work for a time commitment. The hours may be during the day or at night depending on which group of people the marketing company is looking for.

The tricky part is getting on the list to be called. Sometimes marketing companies place ads in local papers looking for people to be members of the focus group. Sometimes they call up people who have responded to market surveys in the past.

Mystery Shoppers

Mystery shoppers fulfill a role much like paid survey takers. They give a business valuable feedback on performance. In fact, the feedback is so valuable the business will pay to get it. The kind of information the companies want are all factors you would consciously or unconsciously pick up anyway. For instance, a restaurant should be clean, pleasant, seats you as fast as it can, and delivers value for the dollar.

Of course, any business that offers its services or is open to the public is fair game for this job. Like the paid survey opportunities, finding these opportunities is mostly about finding the marketing companies and other businesses that are willing to pay consumers to provide this service. Think in terms of restaurants and retailers in particular.

Like the paid survey option, the key is to do the research on marketing companies. In addition some of the hints for looking for any other part-time job also apply. Some of these opportunities will never be advertised so networking can be key. The other thing to do is to keep an eye out for print and online want ads. In addition, **www.mysteryshop.org** is a website with resources including how much the assignments pay. The term to look for is customer satisfaction services. There are also books on the subject. One is by Jim Erskine *Dining for Dollars*, as well as *The Mystery Shopper's Manual* by Cathy Stucker.

Again, like the marketing surveys, think in terms of hours and dollars in the range of a couple hours and $20 and under for assignments. Of course, if you did it on your own and had five assignments that paid $20 an hour plus any merchandise your purchased as an added bonus, it might be a great opportunity.

Like other options, the time commitment has to be evaluated against the income and the start up costs. In particular, be wary of any opportunity that requires you to spend money to make money. The object is to raise cash not spend it.

Telephone Book Deliveries

Every year, telephone book companies are faced with a problem. For the advertisers message to get out, the phone book must be delivered. Some telephone directory companies will place ads on bulletin boards in local papers looking for delivery drivers.

This is a short-term job measured in days not months. The pay will probably be competitive with other part-time jobs. However, it can be a great way to make some cash. It will require having a car or access to a car. In addition, the telephone company will want to see that you have a good driving record and that you have insurance.

The trick with this job is to combine it with other aspects of your search for quick cash. While you're out delivering the phone books, carry a 3 by 5 card or memo pad so you can jot down opportunities you may encounter. This job, like temping, is almost bound to introduce you to people and places you would not ordinarily encounter. So keep your eyes open for help wanted signs if you're looking for a job. If you're a freelancer, keep your eye out for markets for your services. If you're unemployed, keep your eye out for places that look like they do something close to what your old employer did.

Pet Care Giver

One of the biggest problems people have with pets is who is going to walk them and care for them while the owners are away. Becoming a dog walker or pet sitter can be a great source of extra cash. Be prepared to think through and address issues such as liability and insurance. In addition, anytime you're going into people's houses, security issues for them and you are likely to present themselves. For example, don't be offended if people ask you for a background check. Also, expect to produce evidence that you are bonded. In addition, you will need to comply with local business registration requirements, such as permits, fees, and licenses.

You should do your own informal background checks on potential clients as well. You certainly have a right to say no to any customer or animal that presents a risk to your person. The easiest way to avoid problems with customers in the long run is to avoid the problematic ones in the short run.

Your insurance agent should be able to help you with a personal bond as well. Since you'll be providing a service for hire, you should think through how much you'll charge and make sure customers know how much the service is and what services you'll provide. For example, will you also pick up their mail and water plants?

Two excellent resources on getting started in the business are the *National Association of Professional Pet Sitters* at **www.petsitters.com**, 800-296-pets and *Pet Sitters International* at **www.petsit.com**, 800-268-sits. Joining them may be as source of referrals as well. In general though, people seem to find pet sitters as they find other service providers. First they exhaust their free sources of family and friends; then they ask their family and friends for people they know who do it. And finally, they ask their vets, check the Yellow Pages, and go online. Since this will probably be a referral-based business, it may pay to cultivate vets, pet stores, and grooming services.

Line Stander

Celebrities don't generally stand in line for themselves. You may not be able to immediately come up with a job as the personal assistant to a mega-watt media type, but that doesn't mean the willingness to wait can't serve your cash needs. In Washington D.C., for example, lobbyists face a problem. Their time is too valuable for them to wait in line for congressional hearings that they need to attend. The solution offered by Congressional Services Company is to pay others to wait in line for the lobbyists. Estimates of compensation runs as high as $10 to $20 an hour. However, many ordinary people will pay to avoid waiting in the dreaded Department of Motor Vehicles line.

This particular opportunity contemplates standing in line to do shopping and drop off items as well as pick them up. Some people also make money by offering to wait in people's houses for the cable guy and other repair people.

If you decide to do this to raise cash, the same issues that apply to taking care of animals also need to be addressed. Make sure you have insurance and bonding. Set the fees clearly and in writing from the very beginning.

The other thing to be aware of is that the person hiring you has to provide absolutely clear instructions beforehand to the service person on exactly what they want. You do not want to be in the business of negotiating premium cable packages or home repairs. Your job is to wait, let the person in, and let them out.

USING YOUR CREATIVITY AND TALENT

This section discusses several ways you might be able to earn cash by tapping into your creativity and knowledge to raise money quickly. This strategy is as old as the idea of minstrels who used to sing for their supper. If you can make the only truly cute leprechaun for Saint Patty's Day out of crepe paper, chicken wire, and green food dye, this might be the time to start considering doing it for profit.

Just as people's talents and interests are wide and far ranging, so are the possibilities for profiting from creativity and talent. This is as area where doing some soul searching may pay off very well. Almost everyone has some unique talent or ability that could potentially be harnessed to generate some quick cash.

Of course, having the talent is only part of the process. At some point, the talent and creativity will have to be marketed and sold. Some people hate this part of using these ideas to raise cash; others can't wait to start calling people. It pays to know which group you're in before you start. It also pays to remember that while not everybody likes or is good at every task that is essential to make a project successful, it's often possible to find a friend who will complement your skills so that if you work together you can succeed.

Arts and Crafts

Stories abound of people who needed money and had nothing to sell until they came up with a clever concept. Many people raise cash by making arts and crafts and selling them. Without a doubt, the most important question you should answer before you even think of trying to make money on crafts is this—do I like it enough to do this for free? Second—do I have time and money to lose if nobody buys this?

This is not an option for everyone. But it might definitely be an option for you. The first step is to identify your market. Remember, your objective here is generating cash quick. If this foray works and you decide you want to do more of it, then you should do some serious and hard thinking about what it is you like to do and what it is that you would do well. Many people who are good at crafts gravitate into selling them in a long and drawn out process.

However, if you are doing this to generate cash quickly, then you want to come up with somewhere to sell the item long before you make it. Doing crafts for quick cash will only work if it's something you can produce ultra cheaply and sell easily and quickly.

If you want to do it as an ongoing business, then low costs and knowing where to sell it may not be as important as it is if you only want to make a quick buck. Think more like a garage sale than *Martha Stewart*. To that end, ask yourself what you have an abundance of already that you could quickly sell. For example, some farmers paint old tractor parts matte black and sell them off as lawn ornaments. Other people who lived near cornfields make corn dolls.

There are many books that can help you with this. Anything by Barbara Brabec on crafting, especially *Creative Cash: How To Profit From Your Special Artistry, Creativity, Hand Skills And Related Know-How* and Reader's *Digest Back To Basics: How To Learn And Enjoy Traditional American Skills* as well as Reader's Digest *Crafts & Hobbies: A Step-By-Step Guide To Creative Skills* are all good resources to start with. The National Craft Association at **www.craftassoc.com/hobby bookcontents.html** and Barbara Brabec at **www.barbarabrabec.com** have websites with additional resource information.

Nothing breeds creativity like an urgent need for cash flow. Just as the early American pioneers were skilled and resourceful at using what they could find easily, modern crafters are also very ingenious. Craft items range in complexity from simply things like these to intricate and time-consuming projects. The key is finding something you can make that other people will buy, that you can charge enough for to make it worthwhile.

The point is the same, first you need to ask yourself where it can be sold, then you need to think and work incessantly on where it can be sold inexpensively.

Promoting Your Crafts

Many crafters get started selling their wares during garage sales. This is a pretty easy way to get started. However, this approach will work better if you can do this during a block garage sale, or even better, an all-town garage sale. The more foot traffic that goes by your booth, the better your chances are that people will stop and look. If people stop and look, then some of them should buy your products.

Also consider craft dealers as well as gift shops. They may not offer you as good of a price as what you would get if you sold it directly. But remember this is not as yet a true business idea. This is mostly just a way to raise cash. Yes, you could probably make $200 by selling it on your own, but if your only goal is to raise $100 to send your youngest to camp, you don't want to spend a lot of time doing all the work it may require to sell these products yourself. As for what to make—the sky's the limit on possibilities. Virtually any craft can be sold to the right buyer.

Advertising in the local paper can also be affordable if it's free or low cost. Don't forget many supermarkets and other stores will let you post your items for sale. This is very much selling by appointment as you list your phone number and then set up time to have the callers over and buy the items. This can be a very cost effective way to sell.

Other choices, such as craft shows, craft malls, and craft stores, generally take money to get involved in and may not be a great way for a novice to get started. But if you're absolutely certain you can recover your costs and make the quick cash you need, then its definitely an option.

How long it takes to make money off of craft sales depends entirely on how long it takes to make what you're going to sell. If you're making twisty animals in the basement and you can make thirty every hour, that's going to take a lot less time and materials than if you're making hand carved furniture that takes a month for each piece.

Craft sales may offer a unique way for you to make money off of supplies and creativity you already have available. And chances are if this sections appeals to you at all it appeals because you're already interested in crafts and craft making.

The biggest disadvantage is that if you're looking for truly quick cash, this may be a far cry from what you need to do since you may have to spend money and time you simply don't have available.

You should definitely research this area, particularly if you are at all interested in selling a food product. Food sales to consumers are among the most strictly regulated business transactions there are. Also, if you're going to sell individual products to consumers that may hurt them, you definitely need to be aware of product liability laws and their potential effect on you.

There are a host of legal concerns that come into play with starting a craft business. There are federal regulations governing craft rules as well as labor laws about what can be produced legally in homes. In addition, crafters who sell to the public should have insurance and collect sales tax. Finally, many different intellectual property issues come up with craft business. Part of this requires good business planning so you don't loose any rights over your creations. Over aspects of operating the craft business require you to respect other people's intellectual property as well.

With all of these craft sales options, check with your city and county ordinances as well as state and federal laws and regulations for any needed permits or other licenses. If making the craft appears to be set to take off, *products liability insurance* is definitely something to also look into.

Writing for Fun and Profit

This section shows ways you may be able to make some relatively fast cash by selling articles to magazines and websites. It doesn't cover books, because unless you're Steven King, it's going to be hard to generate cash from writing books quickly.

There are writing opportunities out there that could be the solution to a need for quick cash. Magazine articles might indeed help generate quick cash for you under some circumstances. However, writing is like many crafts. If you're doing it for money, then the first question is who will buy it. Ideally, like with crafts, you will sell your work before it's written. Although, if you are an unknown writer and it may be a challenge—it should be your goal.

Many people are afraid to write articles to make money because they fear the research. One of the top selling article categories on the web and in print is the *how to* article. If you are a tax accountant who has a second home and you had a problem with deductibility issues you have an article.

One of the harder things to do in writing is to establish your credibility with the audience. If you are a realtor and you write an article for a magazine on how to sell your house, then you should have instant credibility with the reader. This is crucial because it can make the difference between an article that sells once and one that can be resold. Many magazines want an agreement with you that say they and only they can use the article after you sell it to them. However, as a writer if you can get a different kind of contract, you can keep selling the article derived money from it over and over. This, of course, lets you make more money than if you can only sell it once.

Magazine articles are not the only possibilities either. They are merely the most obvious. The real money may be made in the more specialized opportunities available to the intrepid and successful freelance writer. Businesses are huge consumers of writing talent for everything from speeches to annual reports. Marketing alone consumes business letters, brochure, trade show handouts, and article for the trade press as well as the staple of the news release. CEOs gain much benefit and a boost in reputation by having articles published. But they may or may not have any interest in or ability to write them themselves. Again the first question is "Who can I sell this service to?" Then the question is "What writing product can I sell?"

For example, if you were a talented speech writer who needed cash quickly, consider heading to the library to get *The Well-Fed Writer* by Peter Bowerman. Speech writing is a specific form of writing for hire, and it can pay well. Although Bowerman's book is designed more for prose writers than speechwriters, the sections on how to market writing services are very good.

Another book that might be worth a look at is *Speech Is Golden: How To Sell Your Wit, Wisdom, Expertise and Personal Experiences on the Local and National Lecture Circuit* by Gerald Gardner. Although this book is designed for the person who will be doing the actual speaking, it gives a very good overview of what is necessary to deliver a speech that's good enough to get paid for.

An opportunity similar to the greeting card caption idea is the possibility of submitting humorous stories to magazines. You'll need to check individual magazines, but *Reader's Digest* and *Family Handyman* both buy stories. *Family Handyman* pays $100 per story. They are interested in funny stories that have to do with home improvement projects gone astray. It's a very long shot, but it might work—at 37 cents for postage, it's certainly a tempting possibility. *Family Handyman* submissions become their property. Send the articles to:

The Family Handyman
2915 Commers Drive, Suite 700
Eagan, MN 55121

Sewing

Sewing can be a potent cash generator. You'll want to check with your local branch of government because some states have labor laws that prohibit hiring people to make certain things in the home such as food, wearing apparel, toys and dolls, and certain other products. Your state Department of Labor can tell you for sure if your state has such a law. But nonetheless you may be able to make small and not so small amounts of money by doing basic mending and alterations.

Teach a Class

Almost any skill you have is fair game to teach. Chances are, if it's something that is working out in your life or some specialized piece of knowledge you have acquired, you can *teach* it for profit. This can be as formal as going to a university, college, or community college or as simple as calling up a community center.

Another resource you should be aware of is the option of teaching at an independent learning center. Sometimes there are very well paid, sometimes they are not paid at all, so check it out before you go. Even if it is unpaid, you may make some great networking contacts or find a market where you could sell your work. People with advanced degrees in certain areas may be able to retread aspects of their background into a useful seminar people will pay money to go to.

A survey through the local community college catalog of not for profit classes should raise any number of possibilities. Some perennial favorites are investments, cooking, dance, and computer skills. Remember, this process of getting and fulfilling teaching jobs will work better if you can market to who you are. For example, if you are single and have no children, a getting into the better preschools class might not work. On the other hand, if you are a real estate person who lives in their third Victorian house, a class on restoring Victorian houses for fun and profit might work very well.

Think in terms of industries and concepts that you are already familiar with. For example, if you have a business remodeling kitchens and bathrooms. You are a natural for a seminar on getting the most bang for your remodeling buck. Many trades people make tidy profits on the side by giving homeowners basic knowledge of repairs they can do easily and what repairs need professionals. Usually, these classes are taught by professionals who also do the services they're teaching about as well. So if you know how to do a skill now may be the time to see if you can teach a class in it.

Tutor

Tutoring just means teaching a class for one. People make money teaching everything from math to German to cooking one on one. There is every reason in the world to think you might be able to do this. Though this is generally more of a one on one arrangement than teaching a class. The sections on marketing may be helpful in figuring out how to get this option going as well. *Tutoring as a Successful*

Business: An Expert Tutor Shows You How by Eileen Kaplan Shapiro may be worth looking at.

Anybody interested in this strategy should look at the freelancing sections because it raises the same issues as other self-employment routes to quick cash. You will have to pay taxes including self-employment taxes on what you make. In addition, like all of the business-based strategies the potential risks and rewards need to be evaluated carefully. For example, you can't do a Yellow Pages ad with your home phone; you need a business phone. Business phones generally cost more than residential phones. (Use the materials in Chapter 2 to make a careful and reasoned choice.)

Of course, advertising can be done on a shoestring as well. If you choose to you could just mail out flyers to local schools and post your card in the local supermarket. These are very low cost ways to get the word out.

Consult

Chances are if one employer paid you once to acquire or use knowledge, it's possible that another employer might also pay you for it. If you can solve problems for businesses or have skills they need you may be able to work out a deal with them to hire you as a *consultant*.

However, this is basically an employment strategy. You generally won't get paid until you do the work. In addition, your compensation may be tied to the success of the advice that you give. It can work better in high tech where you may have a certain expertise that is needed on a job or where the team in place needs the skill but doesn't want to hire someone to do it. They may be willing to hire you as a consultant to bring your special knowledge to bear on the problem.

If you are even slightly interested in this as a strategy to raise quick cash, you should read the section on freelancing carefully. First and foremost you must answer the question of how much money you need to raise and where you can get it. Like writing, antiques, and garage sales, the crucial question is where will you sell it?

BECOME A LANDLORD

The idea of taking in borders to pay the rent is a pretty old one. It may be the solution to your cash flow problems particularly if you find yourself in a situation where you are land rich and cash poor. This is, however, one of the trickier ways to raise cash out floor. Successfully renting out part of your house depends on several factors. Some of them are internal and have to do with you and some of them are purely external and have to do with the house, community rules, and norms.

The specifics are pretty straightforward. If you have a house that can be easily shared you could rent out part of it and live in part of it your-self. The perfect scenario would be if you had purchased a two flat apartment. Whether you planned on converting it into a large single occupancy but ran out of cash, or bought it with the plan of renting out a unit, this could be a great source of money. Many people get started in the residential real estate business by buying a two flat, living in one unit and renting out the other.

Generally, a structure that was already approved for rental housing would meet the code requirements for the safety and construction needs of the building. Plus, unless the zoning requirements of the place you live in changed then you should not have any problems with this.

The further you move away from that set of circumstances, the more you have to think about this strategy. For example, a two flat is usually a completely separate apartment with its own exit and entrance, bath, toilet, and cooking facilities. If pursuing this option would require you to share your own bath and kitchen, give it serous thought as to whether you are the sort of person who can do this. Some people would rather share their toothbrush than their kitchen with a stranger—let alone the bathroom. However, other people are completely indifferent as to whom they live with.

Give serious thought as to what the house rules will be—both for yourself and for your tenant. If you are an amateur bird watcher whom dreams of being up every morning at 4:30 a.m., then don't rent to a heavy metal band and expect it to go well.

Also aside from any of these factors you must be prepared for the legal and business requirements that go into renting property. Are you prepared to collect rent and more importantly, to evict people if they don't pay? The worst of all worlds would be to lose space and privacy only to find out you got a deadbeat who is not going to pay. There is a certain kind of tenant that never pays they just move from place to place for as long as it takes to get evicted. You should be prepared to have tenant-screening procedures. Secondly, you should join or consider attending landlord investor groups. As a small landlord you will generally be exempt from many rental requirements. However, many does not mean all. Additionally, you will be getting income from rental property. This means you have to be prepared to report it on your taxes. Last but certainly not least you should have a heart to heart with your insurance agent to be sure you're covered for renting the property.

You should also familiarize yourself with all the applicable state and federal housing laws that are going to apply. The federal *Fair Housing Act* and the EPA's lead-based paint rules immediately come to mind. Next, you must take a crash course in landlord law for the state you live in. Landlord groups and associations can help you. Local city government may also have landlord tenant ordinances you must become familiar with. You'll also want to check zoning and housing laws to make sure you can rent. Finally, state and federal rules generally control acceptable uses of information obtained in background checks and credit reports. If you live in a condominium, you should definitely check the association by-laws to see if renting it out is even an option. Many associations have very strict rules regarding renting out condos.

Renting out your spare room or spare house has to make sense economically. Repairs you might let go, often have to be made when a tenant is living there. If the place is just too expensive for you to maintain, consider moving out and renting a cheaper apartment.

So after you've added up the rent for a year, take out all the expenses. Be careful to include everything and add a cushion for maintained and emergency repairs.

Be sure to get as much money up front as possible. It is far easier to get a tenant than it is to get rid of one. There are websites that can help such as **www.mrlandlord.com**, **www.landlord-tenant-online.com**, **www.rentlaw.com**, and **www.vacancynet.com**.

Find It

7

Of all the ways to raise cash quick, nothing beats finding money that's been lost or misplaced. This chapter looks at ways people can check to see if money is being held for them that they have misplaced or may not even know about. This usually involves contacting state and federal governments. Finding lost cash presents two different legal issues. If you lost it, it merely involves reasserting your prior legal claim to it. If on the other hand you want to go looking for other people's lost valuables, that presents questions of ownership.

This chapter also looks at issues involved in finding lost money and other valuables. The questions of who owns lost property are often questions of state law; however, federal law applies to certain matters such as some Indian artifacts and objects taken from federal lands and historic sites. In many states, the finder of treasures buried in the earth has the best claim on the property—next only to the true owner of the object.

Looking for money you've lost or misplaced is kind of like a treasure hunt you hold for yourself. You may not find anything, but who knows? The following is a quick checklist of places to look that might yield some cash.

◆ Sofas
◆ Car seats and car interiors
◆ Old clothes pockets
◆ The back yard with a metal detector
◆ Keep an eye out on streets
◆ Pay phone and vending machines
◆ Gift Certificates that you can redeem for cash
◆ Birthday and other greeting card piles
◆ Pop cans and other recyclables, as well as bottles with deposits
◆ Under the bleachers at sporting events
◆ Storage lockers from when you moved
◆ Stock options—see if they can be cashed in early
◆ Vacation and sick pay that can be cashed in
◆ Season tickets that can be sold back or redeemed
◆ Club memberships that can be refunded

JUDGMENTS

Though it probably won't be a source of quick cash, you may be involved in a class action suit and not know it. Class action suits were designed so that all the members of a particular group had claims against a defendant or defendants could have their cases heard instead of having to each go to court. However, each year people bring lawsuits, win the court battle, and fail to collect. If you are one of those people who has a judgment that can be enforced, then that may be a source of quick cash.

Generally speaking, the attorneys who are suing the defendants will put considerable effort into notifying you and tracking you down. If you feel that you've been injured and don't recall receiving notice of a class action suit, you can check two websites that may have information. The first is one that tracks class actions involving stock and bonds and other securities at the *Securities Class Action Clearinghouse*. The Clearinghouse is run by Stanford School of Law and can be found at **http://securities.stanford.edu**. The Clearinghouse is primarily designed for lawyers and has a lot of technical information for them. But a fast search of the filings might lead the name of the company you believe injured you. Second, these class action suits attract big name law firms. One of the firms that handles many suits is *Milberg Weiss*. Their cases and info about them are available at their website located at **www.milberg.com**.

If you sue someone and win, you usually get a judgment against them for damages. Sometimes people go through all the trouble of a court action and then don't collect the judgment for whatever reason. If you have sued anyone for anything and you got a judgment for money damages and did not collect it, it could be a source of quick cash. However, there are some considerations you may want to weigh carefully before considering this option for certain types of settlements.

Congress passed a law that changed how settlements were paid out for people who suffered catastrophic and permanent personal injuries.

Many families had difficulties with administering large cash judgments. The families of victims who had been severely injured were receiving large cash settlements at times in their life when they were least able to make rational and effective financial decisions. These were victims who in many cases could simply not support themselves anymore because their injuries were so sever. The large cash settlements they received represented their only option other than public assistance. Yet the families had no experience in figuring out how to invest millions of dollars safely so it generated enough money to pay for the injured person's medical care and other needs throughout the rest of their life. So Congress took action to strongly encourage the payment of *structured settlements* that would pay out the settlement money at a slower amount to ensure the victims and their family's financial security. Many states also passed laws regulating how settlements were paid out.

Having said that, the next way of turning judgments into quick cash is pretty tame but can be quite effective. Let's assume you won a judgment. Your judgment was for $120,000 paid out at a $1,000 a month for ten years. At the time you are ok with that, but things changed and now you could use cash. You have a stream of payments coming in, but you don't need $120,000 in ten years. Now you need $40,000 in a week. There are lenders that will lend you money secured by the stream of future monthly payments of the judgment. Generally, these companies advertise in bar journals. If you want to pursue this option, you should definitely raise it with the attorney who won the judgment for you. He or she may be able to help steer you towards reputable companies.

There are some other alternatives you might want co consider such as if you have been injured and you are suing to recover damages. There are some people who will lend you money against the value of your future judgment. However, these options should be investigated carefully. It's one thing to lend money on a judgment you've already received, its quite another thing to loan money based on the possibility you might win in court. An iron rule is that the more risk the lender takes, the more interest the borrower pays. In this case, the risk is very high, so the interest is likely to be just as high.

UNCLAIMED PROPERTY

Found money can be a lot more than the $5 you put in your ashtray and forgot about. Each year thousands, if not millions of dollars is lost by Americans in the form of gift certificates they never use, utility deposits they forget about, and bank accounts they just never get around to closing. In the very distant past in Great Britain, unclaimed property reverted to the English monarch. In the United States, it actually winds up with the treasurer of your state. In your quest for quick cash, this is definitely a rock you want to turn over.

Luckily, it's never been easier to check if you have unclaimed property. Just go to **www.unclaimed.org**—the website of the *National Association of Unclaimed Property Administrators*. The search is free, fast, and easy. If you are lucky enough to have unclaimed property in a state, you can just follow the website to that state's state treasurer's website. If you want to talk to a real person rather than the Web, you need to call or write to the office of your state treasurer in your own state and any other states you may have lived in.

In addition, there is a private website **www.missingmoney.com**. This site duplicates much of the information that is available on the National Association website. However, one big plus of this site is that it has links to other sites you may wish to search for unclaimed funds. For example, it has links to savings bonds, the IRS, pensions, Department of Housing and Urban Development, FDIC, Veterans Benefits, Swiss Bank Accounts, and unclaimed property in Australia.

Expect to have to fill out lots of paperwork. That will take a bit of time. Think weeks not days, but depending on when you need the money and how much money you need, this could be a great way to raise some quick cash. Plus, best of all, its your money.

Almost everybody who has a need for quick cash dreams of winning the lottery or stumbling across buried treasure in the backyard. The odds of a person having unclaimed money with a state treasurer are considerably better than the chances of getting a winning lottery ticket.

BURIED TREASURE

It has to be mentioned in passing that if you or anyone you know has a metal detector or cheap access to one, now might be the time to fire it up in your quest for quick cash. If you confine your searches for lost treasure to your own backyard you own (as opposed to renting) you should be fine. However, once you venture off property that you clearly own, you should definitely know your legal rights. You should have a written agreement with the owner that spells out exactly what will happen to the items that you discover and how the proceeds will be divided. If you discover archeological items, then state laws may be triggered that protects archeological finds. Just as the federal government protects items found on federal lands, many states have similar statutes that protect items on state lands.

As a general rule, stay off of all federal lands with a metal detector, unless you're prepared to do your homework. Simply possessing a metal detector on certain federal historic sites may implicate you in legal penalties. For example, the Gettysfield Battlefield site is clearly off limits.

As a last point—there are many people doing metal detecting. You may not make a killing at it because the ground is well trod. But on the other hand, you might find enough to make it worth your while.

Part Four
Making the
Right Decision

Quick Cash Cautions

8

Whole industries have grown up to service the need for quick cash. Many of the options in this chapter should be looked at cautiously. Many of them could work to generate some quick cash, but they could cause long term financial complications. People who want to raise cash quickly should especially be wary of the get-rich-quick ads that are often seen on telephone poles, bulletin boards, and the Internet. These often not only produce no cash, but also take away much needed money. Others, like payday loans, will work to generate cash, but the cost of the loan may be prohibitive. Make sure to examine all of your options before settling on a choice that may work, but that you might regret.

PAYDAY LOANS

Chances are you have heard of *payday loans* or seen their signs in strip malls or seen the ads on TV. This is a hot area of personal finance right now, because regulators are eager to pass laws to control the use and abuse of consumers in this areas. Many consumers are eager to get the cash, and the industry is willing and ready to lend.

Some payday loans are available on the web. However, most people who use this service go into a physical facility. It will vary by region, but many of them seem to be located in strip malls.

This loan is, in many ways, the opposite of a real estate mortgage. A real estate mortgage requires reams of paper and signatures. Often residential mortgages require more than a dozen signatures of the person taking out the mortgage and at least that many piles of paper. A payday loan only requires a bank account and a pay stub (as well as identification).

The person gives the *cash shop* a postdated check. For example, if the person wanted to borrow $160, he or she would give the shop a check for somewhere around $200. At the end of the period, the cash shop would deposit the check. The person would get the short-term loan he or she needed and the shop would get the difference between $200 and $160. On $200, $40 would be an effective return of 20% interest for a two-week loan. That's a pretty impressive return when you think that certificates of deposit pay between one and two percent.

If you pay between 10% and 20% per $100 to borrow the money, then the payday loan provider is making a tidy sum on the money. Consumer advocates have been big critics of these loans because if consumers cannot pay the loan, they have to roll it over. Assuming the consumer rolled the loan over for a year, then the APR on annual percentage rate would be quite high. Think in terms of hundreds of percent for the loan. However, in many states, people are limited in their ability to roll the loan over. There's no doubt that a credit union would be a cheaper sources. But as the payday loan industry points out, if you've got so-so credit and no assets, it may be hard to get a loan from a credit union.

It can take as little as fifteen minutes to get the cash in your hand from the brick and mortar store. The web option relies on direct deposit into your checking account so that option will probably take at least one banking day for the cash to arrive. If the loan is for a small amount, the store may advance the cash directly. But if the loan is for a larger amount, then you will probably get a check and have to take it to the bank. Be sure that you find out where the store's bank is located. Generally speaking, if you have a check drawn on an account located in the same bank, you can cash it without any questions asked.

Advantages and Disadvantages

The major advantage to this loan is speed, ease, and a low profile. Fifteen minutes is pretty fast for a loan. The form is pretty easy to fill out. There's generally no credit check, since you're essentially borrowing money from yourself. It's a pretty low profile way to raise cash compared to having a garage sale that all the neighbors can see.

The major disadvantage to this loan is that it is an extraordinarily expensive way to borrow money. However, the biggest risk to this way of raising cash is that by the time most people start hocking the rent money, they have arrived in a rough cash spot. So they borrow on their paychecks or welfare checks to meet an emergency because they don't have the money. Then the loan comes due and they can't pay it, so they start rolling the loans over to avoid having to pay the loans back. This means that the interest keeps mounting up.

This is a very expensive way to borrow money from yourself. If there are any other options it might be wise to look at them. In general loans with co-signers can be troublesome for both parties. If the borrower doesn't pay then the co-signer is on the hook and that can greatly strain the relationship. On the other hand if there were ever a time for a co-signer this might be the time.

SCAMS

The *Federal Trade Commission* (FTC) cracks down on fraudulent business opportunities. A list of their targets pretty well matches a list of ads that are often seen on bulletin boards, telephone poles, and the Internet. These are businesses that allegedly can be started with little or no money and that will generate a $1,000 or more a week from home. The ads usually provide an 800 number or a website that people can go to.

Some of the more common false business opportunities that are used to bilk people out of their money include:

◆ envelope stuffing;
◆ medical billing;
◆ vending machines;
◆ craft assembly work;

◆ stapling booklets;
◆ greeting card display racks; and,
◆ CD-ROM displays.

Just as the World Wide Web has made it possible for many Americans to make their living in ways that would have never been possible in earlier times, it has also spawned more than a few hoaxes, scams, and just plain downright dumb schemes for people to make money.

There are probably as many different Internet scams as there are cons trying to pull them. With any business opportunity that is being offered for purchase, consumers should take certain actions to protect themselves. First of all, during an effort to raise cash quickly, you should be wary of spending any money. The end of the endeavor is to raise money not spend it. Before you spend one dime of your money during a cash crunch, you need iron plated estimates of how much money you can expect to make from this opportunity, and how soon you might realistically expect to make it. A legitimate business opportunity sale should not be shrouded in mystery. You should be able to easily and readily discover fairly good estimates about how much you can expect to make. Second you should evaluate this business as you would any other. In any opportunity, you have to ask yourself what it is that is likely to make you successful in it compared to others. If you can start a successful business like this one, so can everyone else. Expect the competition to be bloody.

Pyramid schemes and chain letters are also usually a waste of time. Chain letter activity can potentially fall under federal laws that prohibit mail fraud. Mail fraud carries significant criminal penalties. The FTC's website at **www.ftc.gov** is one of the best resources for consumers to use to protect themselves from scams.

You should be very skeptical of any mailing or call by a service provider that offers them a guaranteed loan if they pay an advance fees.

CAR TITLE LOANS

A car loan is basically a loan that is made to a borrower that uses a car title as security for payment of the loan. This loan can be acquired fairly easily. First and foremost, you'll need a car for which you hold the title. Pawn shops will even lend on car titles, sometimes. There are sites on the web that offer online services and many of these outlets advertise in the penny saver. In addition, if you keep your eyes out while driving, you'll probably find them as well. These loans are fast—think minutes.

This advantage is that it's fast. The lender will not be as interested in your credit as will many other loan sources. The disadvantage is potentially huge. In the application, sometimes, they will ask for as many as ten references for contact information. This is so they can easily repossess the car and sell it if you don't pay. You run the risk of losing the car, any balance you had built up in it, and your job if you need the car to drive to work.

These loans are regulated by federal laws such as the *Truth in Lending* laws that require a disclosure of the rate and amount of the interest. This is a high risk, very expensive way to raise money. If you fail to pay off the loan, you run the real danger of losing your car.

LOAN SHARKS

Loan sharks are often very willing to lend you money, but it will come at a high rate of interest and perhaps a risk to your personal safety. This is basically an illegal loan. Loaning money to consumers is highly regulated by the federal and state governments. To say the least, loan sharks are not regulated. They operate completely outside the law. In the movies, these are the people threatening to break people's legs if they don't pay up. Like most of the high interest loans in the book, its easier to get into this debt then to get out of it. This is definitely one loan you're better off without.

The advantage, if there can be said to be one for this kind of loan, is that a loan shark will probably lend money. The disadvantage is that the shark may harm you if you don't pay it back.

BARGAIN SALES OF REAL ESTATE AND COLLECTIBLES

It goes without saying that a bargain sale of a collectible is going to be heartbreaking. In addition, many people make a comfortable living off buying distressed real estate. It's usually far easier to sell real estate and collectibles than to get them back. Unfortunately, the sales are final and once the items are gone, they're gone for good. So if you have to sell them quickly, you may wind up with a bad situation where you no longer have the items and you did not get a fair market value price for it.

TAX REFUND LOANS

A *tax refund loan* is like borrowing money from yourself. Assuming you are paying taxes on income from a job and your employer is withholding taxes from it, you should start the tax process with a certain amount of money already ready to pay your income taxes with.

There are certain banks and big chain, professional tax preparation services that will lend you money based on the difference between what your taxes are and what your employer has withheld from your wages and paid into the government. You receive a loan check immediately or in the mail a few days later, depending on the company. The loan is repaid when the refund check from the IRS is actually received.

The process starts like this—you go to a professional tax preparation service and they fill out your income taxes. Then they file your tax return for you. They take your refund, but you get a loan for it immediately. However, the loan is for considerably less than the amount of your tax refund. For example, you'll probably have to spend between $20 and $80 to have the tax preparer do your return. Plus there will be a filing fee for them to submit it to the IRS that will probably be between $20 to $50 dollars. And, then you will have to pay a loan fee.

After you've paid all of the fees, you receive a loan for the difference between your total refund that you have given them, and the fees that get paid for the loan and processing. When the IRS sends out your refund check, the tax preparation service gets repaid the money they lent to the taxpayer.

Without this process, you would go to the tax preparer, pay for filing your return, and then wait for the return. Or you might save even more money by filing the return yourself. The biggest advantage of this way of raising cash quick is that the federal tax refund is your money. You are simply paying a premium to get the money sooner. If you usually pay someone to prepare your taxes anyway this could definitely be a big benefit.

The biggest disadvantage is that you could be paying a lot of money relative to the time and amount of the loan. This can amount to a very short, expensive loan.

Believe it or not, the IRS has one of the most accessible, helpful and easy to use websites in the federal government. Go to **www.irs.gov** for tons of info on taxes and filing. In addition, many local and community groups offer assistance to individuals in filing their taxes.

However, keep a skeptical eye out for service providers disguised as information sources. The website of the IRS is obviously pretty reliable information. Plus, they will help you with electronic filing. In addition, you can also download the IRS forms as well as many of their guides and publications. You should be aware that states also have Departments of Revenue which have helpful information.

• • • • •

Generating cash quickly is a life skill like any other. This means it can most definitely be learned. The strategies in this book are all parts of the recipe for solving life's unexpected cash crunches. By combining these strategies and your own resources, you will be able to discover effective and novel solutions to generating cash quickly—no matter what caused your need.

Glossary

401(k). A retirement plan which allows money to grow tax free until it is withdrawn. A 403(b) is offered by not-for-profit entities.

529 college savings plans. Savings for college related expenses grow tax deferred but are subject to penalties on early withdrawal.

A

antique. An item over 100 years old.

B

bounce protection. A service where bank covers checks that would bounce for a fee that must be paid back within a set time.

break-even analysis. A calculation where costs are measured against profits to determine at what point an activity will recover its costs and be profitable.

C

cash flow. A financial measure of income vs. outgo (i.e., how many dollars there are coming in to cover the dollars going out).

community property. In community property states such as California, property acquired during the marriage is deemed to belong to equally to the husband and wife and is subject to division.

consumer credit protection statues. Broad federal consumer protection statutes containing requirements about consumer credit cost disclosure, restrictions on garnishment, credit repair organizations, credit reporting agencies, equal credit opportunity, debt collection practices, and electronic fund transfers.

consumer finance company. A lending institution that specializes in loans to individuals who often would have difficulty getting loans from a bank.

credit life insurance. Insurance that pays off outstanding loans if the borrower dies before the loan is paid.

credit report. A report that shows all your credit activity that goes through banks and other financial institutions. You may request a copy of it for a fee or if you have been refused credit under the Fair Credit Reporting Act you may receive a free copy of it.

credit score. A number that expresses the likelihood of your repaying a loan on time, composed of several different factors including payment history.

credit union. A lending institution made up of members in a specific geographic location or industry that makes loans to its members.

E

earned income credit. A tax credit from U.S. government based on social security contributions to individuals and families whose earnings fall within eligibility guidelines.

equitable distribution. In equitable distribution states assets are distributed according to the legal principles that attempt a fair and reasonable division.

F

Fair Debt Collection Act. A federal statute that sets minimum standards for behavior for collectors of consumer debts.

fraudulent conveyance. A transfer not made for value but instead done to make it harder for creditors to collect money owed to them.

freelance. A person doing work as an independent contractor and not as an employee and is hired to do a specific job or project.

H

hard moneylenders. Private individuals and companies who make high-risk high cost loans on real estate.

home equity line of credit. A loan secured by the value of the house. This loan allows you to borrow money by placing liens against the value of the equity in your home.

I

interest rate. Usually expressed as APR or annual percentage rate, it is the cost of borrowing money.

intestate. A legal term meaning without a will. State intestacy laws will control what happens to your property at your death if you did not prepare a will.

individual retirement account (IRA). A retirement account like a 401(k) that does not need an employer to set up. You may deposit money into it and let it grow tax-free until it is withdrawn.

O

overdraft protection. A prearranged line of credit that protects account holders from bounced check fees.

P

payday loan. A short-term, expensive cash advance loan based on a paycheck or other check that gives the borrower cash up front based on a postdated check.

pawn. To offer up personal property as collateral for a short-term loan.

private mortgage insurance (PMI). Insurance that pays the lender for costs if you default on your home loan.

probate. A legal process of submitting a will to prove its authenticity and distribute the assets of an estate.

R

reverse mortgage. A transaction where a homeowner borrows against the value of his or her house and then receives monthly payment from the lender while they are alive and living in the house.

S

secured creditor. A creditor who holds collateral that he or she can take possession of and sell if the debtor does not pay.

T

temporary aid to needy families (TANF). The successor program to welfare that provides aid to families and individuals falling within certain economic guidelines.

W

WIC. A government program to benefit woman and children by providing certain benefits including food.

Quick Exercises
Appendix A

Some problems need talk to solve them, some need plans and goals, others need action. Raising cash quick depends on all three. These exercises are designed to help you do all three.

Just as the book is a guide to raising cash quick, these exercises should be quick. Do them quickly, analyze the results, and get moving on solving your money challenge.

Ask For It

Write down twenty people you know at random. Now ask yourself who is the person on the list you would be most likely to give money to and who would be the least. Why or why not? Pick the first five you would be most likely to give money to. There is a psychological principle that we often feel about others as they feel about us. Think of those five people and whether or not they *would* help you out and whether or not they *could*.

So how did it go? Did you write down the people. Who is the best prospect? If you have identified someone, when would the best time be to ask?

Borrow It

List five times you've borrowed money successfully for any purpose. Who did you borrow it from? How much did you borrow? For how long? Did you pay it back? Again, sometimes what worked in the past is the best way to make something work in the future.

Now that you've done the exercise, how does this option look. Have you completed it with all the details? What did the answers say about your history of borrowing. If you have not tried this exercise, do it now.

Sell It

Go around the rooms of your home and look at them. What is the most common thing in each room? What is the least common? What do you think you could sell that you own to raise money? What do you know you could never sell because nobody would pay for it?

Now, do a ten minute search on eBay. Put in the search terms for the object you said everybody would buy. Now do the search for what you said nobody would buy. Compare the notes. Were you right in your guesses or wrong? By how much?

After you've done this exercise, look at your estimates and see whether they appear at all possible.

Earn It

Imagine you've inherited enough money to live on for the rest of your life, but that a bizarre catch requires you to pay someone to employ you for forty weeks a year in the occupation of choice to get the inheritance and that you actually have to go and do the work—

◆ What would you pick to do?

◆ What would you never do?

◆ What would bore you no matter how successful you were at it?

◆ What would be interesting enough to keep you going even if you failed at it often and found it frustrating?

Now, go do it. Next to borrowing, this is probably the most likely option for most people. Get something written down because your enthusiasm for looking for an ideal job has to be higher than it would be to find just any old job. Plus, the part-time option may become a full-time option with many benefits

Find It

◆ Have you ever found money anywhere?

◆ Where was the last place you found it?

◆ What place has always been lucky for you?

Answer these questions and determine the potential.

Resources

Appendix B

This appendix has a list of resources that could be helpful in raising cash. Just as the book features broad strategies such as asking for money or borrowing, this appendix has some key resources. For example, if you're contemplating borrowing money, take a look at the section on credit agencies and the credit score. You could save yourself a lot of money by a fast look at your credit report. Resolving any errors could allow you to save a lot of money on a loan. The *Finding It* website list is particularly valuable. State treasurers would like to return lost property so they've set up a website you can easily search. This site should definitely be a place for you to look.

ASK FOR IT

Resources for temporary aid to needy families can be found at the Center on Budget and Policy Priorities website at **www.cbpp.org.** This site also has info on the earned income tax credit.

Help with housing issues can be found at **ww.nhlp.org**—the national housing law project.

In addition, the Government Services agency offers many pamphlets and guides, some free and other at a fairly low cost, at:

www.pueblo.gsa.gov

A search of applicable government programs can be found at:

www.govbenefits.gov/index.jsp

If you think you've lost out on social security benefits try the Social Security Administration website at:

www.ssa.gov

It's possible the check really was in the mail, you could check the possibility out at:

U.S.P.S.
475 L'Enfant Plaza SW
Washington, DC 20260
800-397-4330
www.usps.gov

Another option could be the U.S. Dept. of Treasury to see if you had a savings bond sent to you that did not make it. The Treasury Department has an online search page at:

www.publicdebt.treas.gov/sav/sbtdhunt.htm

If you think you qualify for veterans benefits it may be worth a survey of the Department of Veterans Affairs Benefits' website at:

www.va.gov

Borrowing It

Credit Bureau 800 numbers and websites

Equifax

800-525-6285

www.equifax.com

Experian

888-397-3742

www.experian.com

Transunion

800-680-7289

Credit scoring info can be found on Fair Isaacs as well as:

www.creditscoring.org

Credit Score Company

FairIsaac

www.fairisaac.com/fairisaac

415-472-2211

Selling it

Directory of Websites for electronic auctions

Amazon   http://s1.amazon.com

eBay	www.eBay.com
Half.com	http://half.eBay.com
Yahoo	http://auctions.yahoo.com

Selling cars

Kelley Blue Book at **www.kbb.com.** This is the most recognizable and often quoted guide to the value of new and used cars.

www.carwizard.com also has information on how much your new or used car may be worth.

Electronic Payment Options

PayPal

www.paypal.com

402-935-2050

Bidpay

www.bidpay.com

c2it

800-200-3841

www.c2it.com

Consumer Protection Organizations
State Attorney General's Office
Your State's Attorney General contact information can be found in the Yellow Pages or by accessing the website of the National Association of Attorneys General Website at:

www.naag.org

Better Business Bureau (BBB) can be reached at **www.bbb.org** use the locator on their website or the Yellow Pages to find a local office.

The Federal Trade Commission (FTC) can be contacted at 877-FTC-HELP (877-382-4357) or **www.ftc.gov.**

National Consumer Law Center has a great website filled with resources on consumer peril at **www.consumerlaw.orgs**.

(eBay, Yahoo and Amazon all have consumer safety pages.)

Earning it
Classes & Entrepreneurship Training Resources
The **Corporation for National & Community Service** website, Brief Case for Success, has tools and resources for financial asset development initiatives at:

www.briefcaseforsuccess.com/olc/pub/
CCI/community/overview.html

SCORE (Service Corp of Retired Executives) 800-634-0245 or go the website at:

www.score.org

Finding It

Go to **www.unclaimed.org**, the website of the National Association of Unclaimed Property Administrators, sorted by state, so you can see if you have any unclaimed property.

Sites for Damaged Currency

If it's recognizable local banks and *Federal Reserve* banks will redeem currency.

www.moneyfactory.com/section.cfm/8/39

Damaged currency can be mailed to:

Department of the Treasury
Bureau of Engraving and Printing
Office of Currency Standards
PO Box 37048
Washington D.C. 20013

Information on Damaged Coins

Only the U.S. mint can redeem coinage. For more information go to:
www.ustreas.gov/education/faq/coins/sales.html#q4

Coins can be mailed to:

US Mint
PO Box 400
Philadelphia, PA 19106

Government Agencies that may have your Money

The **Federal Deposit Insurance Corporation** at **www2.fdic.gov/funds /index.asp** keeps list of financial institution that closed down to try to find lost depositor.

HUD may have some of your money from an insured mortgage and their website is at:

www.hud.gov/offices/hsg/comp/refunds/index.cfm

The **IRS** is charged with mailing out millions of refunds if you never got yours contact the IRS at 800-829-1040 or online at **www.irs.gov**.

Just because your company went out of business does not mean all of your pension necessarily disappeared. **The Pension Benefit Guaranty Corporation** (PBGC) keeps tracks of pensions. Their website is **www.pbgc.gov/search/default.htm**.

The Securities and Exchange Commission Office keeps track of certain money resulting from transactions their office supervises through the Office of Investor Education and Assistance at **www.sec.gov**.

50 Fast Ways
to Raise Cash

Appendix C

This list is a *nifty fifty* list of ideas for raising cash. It's not the only way. You can certainly come up with ideas that are as good or far better than these. This section is designed, however, to help you apply the principles in the book by giving you some real life examples of how you might go about using the ideas in the book to raise cash quickly.

Ask For It

◆ Ask your mom.

◆ Ask your other relatives.

◆ Ask your friends.

Borrow It

◆ Get a mortgage.

◆ Get a second mortgage.

◆ Get a reverse mortgage.

◆ Get a home equity loan.

◆ Get a cash advance.

◆ Apply for a micro loan.

◆ Apply for a credit union loan.

◆ Ask your employer up for a payroll advance.

◆ Borrow against your stocks.

◆ If you are student and you need cash for an emergency, see if your college has an emergency loan program.

◆ If you are a member of a union, see if your union has a loan program for members.

◆ Pawn jewelry, electronics, or tools you don't need or use anymore.

Sell It

◆ Have a garage sale.

◆ Use eBay to sell almost anything.

◆ Use TIAS, the Internet Antique Store, for selling antiques.

◆ Use Amazon to auction things.

◆ eBay's Half.com is the perfect place to sell all those CDs and books you've collected.

◆ Sell the extra car or bike.

◆ Sell the boat, trailer, or motorcycle.

◆ Sell the hot wheels collection.

◆ Sell the GI Joe collection.

◆ Sell the comic book collection.

◆ Sell the baseball cards.

◆ Sell the walnut tree in the back yard—don't laugh, a good walnut is worth serious dollars.

◆ Sell the excess hobby tools you bought years ago.

◆ Consign the truly chic outfits you bought, but never wore.

◆ Find the antiques and sell them and find the collectibles and sell them too.

◆ Egg sales if you're female young and healthy can be very well paid.

Earn it

◆ Get a second job.

◆ Get a third job.

◆ Ask your employer for a raise.

◆ Ask your employer for overtime.

◆ Make and sell crafts.

◆ Get a paper route.

◆ Deliver phone books.

◆ Shovel snow.

◆ Freelance.

◆ Temp.

◆ Get a holiday job as a wrapper.

◆ Barter some service you are now paying cash for so you can use the cash for something else.

Find it

◆ Tear the sofa apart.

◆ Tear the car cushions apart.

◆ If you live in a state with a bottle deposit law (California, Connecticut, Delaware, Iowa Maine, Massachusetts, Michigan, Oregon, and Vermont) there's money in returnable bottles, if not there's money in recycling aluminum cans.

◆ Look in all your old books.

◆ Check all your old wallets.

◆ Check all the old piggy banks.

◆ Rent a metal detector and go over your yard.

What Not to Do
Appendix D

One sure and nearly foolproof way to increase dramatically the stress of having to raise cash is to compound the anxiety by breaking a law or doing something unwise. This section deserves a look and review. You want to be sure all your efforts to raise cash do not cause you any problems once the immediate crisis is over. This section gives a broad overview of ten things that are bad ideas. In addition, there is a list of items that should not be sold because those who sell them run the risk of legal entanglements.

10 Things You Should Not Do to Raise Cash In A Hurry

1 Sell anything that doesn't belong to you.
2 Sell something that belongs to an estate before the executor or administrator has clearly passed title to you as the heir.
3 Sell a marital asset without the court's permission.
4 Sell things that infringe on intellectual property that belongs to other people such as their copyrights trademarks and patents.

5 Sell any antique-looking object or collectible without checking to see what it is worth.

6 Lie to get loans.

7 Agree to outrageous interest rates without shopping around.

8 Borrow from family and loved ones if you know you cannot or will not repay them.

9 Cheat the IRS.

10 Sell Indian artifacts, dead stuffed birds, liquor, firearms, blasting powder or devices, or pornography without knowing exactly what you are doing and what all the rules are.

Things You Should Not Sell as an Individual or Should Not Sell without Checking

This list serves as a guide to items that may cause you problems if you try to sell them. For example, federal law imposes stiff penalties for selling any archaeological object that was illegally removed from federal, Indian, state, or private land. If you're planning on selling any on this list, you should be absolutely certain you know all the laws and regulations that apply to their sale.

◆ Alcohol products
◆ Canisters of welding gas
◆ Certain rare and endangered animals
◆ Counterfeit currency and stamps unless you are clearly selling them as forgeries for sale as forged items of interest
◆ Credit cards
◆ Descramblers for cable and satellite
◆ Drugs and drug paraphernalia

◆ Embargoed goods—certain goods may not legally be sold in the United States if they come from countries the U.S. has under an embargo.

◆ Firearms

◆ Fireworks

◆ Human organs—human eggs however may be sold

◆ Identification cards such as ones from state and federal governments

◆ Indian or other cultural artifacts

◆ Knives and other weapons

◆ Locksmithing tools

◆ Pesticides

◆ Pornography depending on applicable rules and laws

◆ Prescription drugs

◆ Products that infringe on other peoples intellectual property or help other people do so

◆ Raw milk

◆ Recalled items

◆ Slot machines

◆ Stolen property of any kind

◆ Stuffed birds

◆ Surveillance equipment

◆ Tickets for events for more than their face value depending on your state

Collectible
Checklist
Appendix E

You probably have more collectible items than you think you do. eBay and other auction sites are great ways to sell them. This list should identify some possibilities. The best way to use it is to photocopy it, put it on a checklist, and walk through your home making a note of any items that appear on it. Then you can begin checking those items in earnest.

A-Z Antiques and Collectibles *Possibility* Checklist

- ☐ Advertising
- ☐ Art
- ☐ Books
- ☐ Bottles
- ☐ Buttons
- ☐ Comic books
- ☐ Crafts
- ☐ Depression glass
- ☐ Etchings
- ☐ Furniture
- ☐ Games
- ☐ Glassware
- ☐ Hummel figures
- ☐ Indians (as in a cigar store)
- ☐ Jewelry
- ☐ Keepsakes or family heirlooms
- ☐ Knick knacks
- ☐ Literary works
- ☐ Letters from famous people
- ☐ Movie collectibles, such as posters and props
- ☐ Nautical maps
- ☐ Oriental rugs
- ☐ Pens—fountain and ink pens
- ☐ Quilts
- ☐ Radios
- ☐ Razors
- ☐ Shaving mugs

- ☐ Sheet music
- ☐ Telephones
- ☐ Toys
- ☐ Umbrellas
- ☐ Valentines Day's cards
- ☐ Video games
- ☐ Watches
- ☐ Xylophones (and other old musical instruments)
- ☐ Yokes (and other farm implements and tools)
- ☐ Zany, old party noisemakers and decorations

Index

401(k), 6, 7, 49, 58, 88, 89, 90, 93, 127, 142
403(b), 89
529 college plans, 130, 131

A

AARP, 78
action steps, 23
adjustable rate mortgages, 72
administrative assistant, 13
ads, 124
advance payment option, 53
AIDS, 132
alimony, 8
Amazon.com, 107
America's Second Harvest, 55
annual percentage rate, 190
antiques, 97, 101, 102
    cleaning, 103
    selling, 104, 105
Antiques Roadshow, 97, 101, 112

appraisals, 74
arts and crafts, 164, 165
ask for it, 37
At the Auction, 123
auctions, 110, 117
    brick and mortar, 123
    dangers on Internet sites, 118, 119, 120, 122
awards, 6

B

back pay, 6
balloon mortgages, 79
bank accounts, 183
bankruptcy, 61, 98
banks, 62, 64, 65, 66, 68, 69, 78, 79, 83, 86, 129
bargain sales, 195
bartering, 14
bill collectors, 59
blood, 132

bonded, 162
bonds, 10
bonuses, 6
book picking, 100
borrow it, 57
bounce protection, 69
break-even analysis, 31
brokerage accounts, 90, 91
budgeting, 21
    analysis, 29
buried treasures, 179, 184, 185

C

capacity, 37
capital gains, 90, 127
car title loans, 86, 93, 194
cash, 63
cash advances, 16, 94, 95
cash flow, 21, 22, 41, 64, 66, 78,
    81, 84, 86, 90, 92
    analysis, 23
cash value, 87, 88
cat sitter, 161
chain letters, 193
character, 63
charge cards, 94
charities, 53
checking accounts, 68
Chicago Creative Investors
    Association, 79
child care, 154
children, 50
children services, 51
closing costs, 74

club memberships, 180
co-workers, 4
collateral, 57, 58, 63, 65, 66, 78,
    79, 82, 83, 84, 90, 92
collateral lenders, 66, 81
collateral loans, 93
collectibles, 97, 100, 101, 102
    bargain sales, 195
    cleaning, 103
    selling, 104, 105
college savings plans, 130, 131
commercial loans, 60
commission, 106
community college, 172
community property, 7
compensation, 4
Congressional Services Company,
    162
consignment, 105
consulting, 146, 173
Consumer Credit Protection Act,
    58
consumer finance companies, 83,
    85, 86, 87
consumer lending, 58
contracts, 61, 148
cost-benefit principles, 25
Coverdell IRAs, 130, 131
crafts, 164, 166, 167
creativity, 163, 165
credit bureaus, 71, 74
credit cards, 94
    advances, 86
credit laws, 58
credit life insurance, 86

credit report, 74, 87
credit score, 63, 64, 65, 66, 70, 71,
    78, 81, 84, 85, 86, 90
credit unions, 62, 64, 65, 66, 68,
    86, 191
creditors, 30, 31, 62
cybercriminals, 120

D

death, 9, 11, 43
death pension, 47
Department of Agriculture, 47, 50
Department of Housing and
    Urban Development, 75, 77,
    184
Department of Motor Vehicles,
    162
Department of Veteran Affairs, 47
Departments of Revenue, 198
Digital Press Collector's Guide,
    102, 111
disability insurance, 86
divorce, 6, 7, 8
dog walker, 161
doing business as certificate, 145

E

early withdrawal penalty, 89
earn it, 137
earned income credit, 52
eBay, 42, 97, 100, 101, 104, 107,
    108, 109, 110, 112, 113,
    114, 115, 116, 117, 118
    feedback, 115

fees, 112
    payment, 114
    regulations, 114
educational IRAs, 130, 131
effort, 28
eggs, 132, 134
Elance, 150
electronic benefits transfer, 49
emergencies, 49
emergency loan programs, 13
emotion, 29
employee deferred tax investment
    plan, 88
employers, 4, 6
energy, 29
envelope stuffing, 192
Equal Credit Opportunity Act, 73
equitable distribution, 7
equity, 76
escrow services, 122
estate, 98
estate planning, 76
evaluating plans, 25
expectations, 29

F

Fair Credit Reporting Act, 73
Fair Debt Collection Act, 59
Fair Housing Act, 73, 176
Fair Isaac, 71
family, 38, 39, 40, 59, 61, 86
family services, 51
FDIC, 184
Federal Reserve, 58

Federal Trade Commission, 58, 77, 192, 194
feedback, 119
FHA loans, 42, 74
FICO, 71
financial aid, 13
find it, 179
first–time home purchase, 130
flea markets, 106
focus groups, 158
food pantries, 43, 54
food sales, 167
food stamps, 47, 48, 49, 53
foreclosure, 78
fraudulent conveyances, 61
free shopper, 124
freelancing, 143, 144, 145, 146, 147, 148, 149
   business planning, 151, 152
   websites, 150
friends, 38, 39, 40, 59, 60, 61
funeral benefits, 47

G

garage sales, 125, 126, 166
gift certificates, 180, 183
gifts, 37, 38
goal setting, 23
government programs, 38, 42, 53, 77
grace period, 95
greeting card display racks, 193
guide books, 100
Guinea Pigs Get Paid, 158

H

Half.com, 116, 117
hammer price, 123
hard money mortgage loans, 79
HIV, 132
hoaxes, 193
holiday pay, 6
home equity loans, 16, 67, 129
hot lunch program, 50

I

identity theft, 108, 120
independent contractor, 143, 147, 148, 149
independent learning centers, 171
informal agreements, 60
inheritance, 10
interest rate, 10, 70, 72, 79, 86, 95
internal assets, 132
Internet Fraud Complaint Center, 116
IRAs, 14, 128, 129
   penalties, 129
IRS, 15, 52, 53, 129, 184, 196, 197
   form 1099, 149
   form SS-8, 149
   form W-2, 148
   form W-5, 53
   Notice 97-60, 15
   Publication 1779, 147
   Publication 596, 52
   Schedule C, 148

J

job loss, 4, 44
job-hunting, 5
joint accounts, 9, 10
joint tenancy, 9
judgments, 181, 182, 183

K

Kelley's Blue Book, 102
knowledge, 163
Kovel's, 101, 102, 104, 111

L

landlord, 174, 175, 177
lenders, 58
life insurance, 10, 58, 86, 87, 88, 93
line of credit, 67, 92
line stander, 162
loan sharks, 86, 195
loans, 57, 60
lost, 179
lump sum death benefit, 46

M

magazine articles, 169, 170
mail fraud, 194
margin loans, 92
marital assets, 7, 8, 98
marriage, 16
Medicaid, 53
medical billing, 192
medical subject, 157

membership fees, 5
Migratory Bird Act, 102
Milberg Weiss, 181
military, 80
misplaced, 179
Mompreneurs, 17
moonlighting, 144
mortgage, 70, 72, 73, 74, 75, 76, 78, 79, 93, 129, 190
My Rich Uncle, 15
mystery shoppers, 159

N

National Association of Professional Pet Sitters, 162
National Association of Unclaimed Property Administrators, 183
National Center for Home Equity Conversion, 77
National Consumer Law Center, 70
Native American art, 103
networking, 5, 156
no income/no asset loans, 78, 79
nonmarital assets, 8
nonprobate assets, 10

O

odd jobs, 157
ordinary income, 101
outplacement benefits, 4, 5
overdraft protection, 67, 69
overtime, 154
ownership, 179

P

parental rights, 133, 135
part-time jobs, 154, 156
    best employers, 155
    worst employers, 155
partnering, 16
pawnbroker, 82
pawning, 57, 66, 81, 82, 83, 85,
    86, 93, 194
payable on death, 9
payday loans, 69, 83, 189, 190,
    191, 192
PayPal, 114, 115
penny stocks, 91
pensions, 10, 93, 94, 184
personal days, 6
pet care giver, 161
Pet Sitters International, 162
phishing, 120
plant closings, 44
plasma, 132, 133
prime rate, 89
prizes, 6
probate, 10, 98
products liability insurance, 168
promissory note, 59
property division, 7, 8
provenance, 103
pyramid schemes, 193

Q

qualified higher education
    expenses, 15, 130

R

recyclables, 180
redirecting expenses, 32
refinancing, 70, 71, 72, 73, 79,
    129
renting, 174, 175, 176
research, 100
research assistant, 13
retirement, 15
reverse mortgage, 75, 76, 77
revolving line of credit, 67
room and board, 15
Roth IRAs, 14, 128
    penalties, 129

S

scams, 192, 193
school, 13
season tickets, 180
Section 8 housing, 53
secured creditors, 30
secured loans, 57
Securities Class Action
    Clearinghouse, 181
security interest , 70
self-employed, 65, 78, 148
sell it, 97
selling, 97, 99
semen, 132, 133
settlements, 181, 182
settling accounts, 6
severance, 4, 5
sewing, 171

shipping costs, 121
sick pay, 6, 180
signature loan, 84
Small Business Association, 152
Small Business Development
    Center, 153
So You Wanna, 158
Social Security benefits, 10, 46, 53
Special Supplemental Nutrition
    Program for Women, Infants
    and Children (WIC), 50
spending, 30
Square Trade, 116
stapling booklets, 193
starting a business, 12
starting a family, 16
state treasurer, 184
stay-at-home, 17
stock, 91, 127
stock options, 180
storage lockers, 180
structured settlements, 182
student loans, 42
student teaching, 13
students, 13
survivor's benefits, 46
Swiss Bank Accounts, 184

T

talent, 163
tax credits, 52
tax refund loans, 196, 197
taxes, 52, 77, 90, 101, 129, 131,
    148, 168

teaching, 171, 172
telephone book deliveries, 160
temping, 138, 139, 140
    disadvantages, 141, 142
Temporary Aid to Needy Families
    (TANF), 51
term insurance, 87
The Dollar Stretcher, 17
The Internet Antique Store
    (TIAS), 104, 111
transitions, 3
Travelers Aid Society, 55
Truth in Lending Act, 58, 87, 195
tuition, 15
    waivers, 13
tutoring, 14, 172

U

unclaimed property, 183
unemployment compensation, 4,
    43, 44, 45
unsecured creditors, 30
unsecured loans, 57
utility deposits, 183

V

vacation pay, 6, 180
vending machines, 192
veterans, 80
    benefits, 47, 184
    loans, 74, 80, 81
volunteer income tax assistance
    program (VITA), 53

W

WIC, 50
work for hire, 149
work-study, 13
writing, 168, 169, 171

Y

Yahoo.com, 107

About the Author

Rich Schell is a lawyer, small farm owner, and author. He grew up in Polo, Illinois in a farming family. His first attempts to raise cash quickly involved weeding thistles and selling pumpkins. Later forays into cash acquisition have involved activities as diverse as mausoleum sales and freelance writing.

He has an extensive background in publishing, including writing, editing, and author representation. He writes and speaks frequently on legal issues involving intellectual property, agricultural entrepreneurship, and immigration. His publications include: *U.S. Immigration and Citizenship Q&A* (co-author), *The Illinois Legal Guide to Direct Farm Marketing*, and *A Study Guide for Criminal Law and Procedure*. He has also written numerous articles on topics including publishing contracts, business entities, and regulatory issues for small farmers.

He holds a B.A. in History and English from Illinois Wesleyan University and a J.D. from Southern Illinois University. He has studied International Law at the University of Notre Dame, London Law Campus. A member of the *Chicago Bar Association* and the *Chicago Creative Investors Association*, he is also currently Secretary *of The Chicago Farmers* and sits on the board of *IDEA* (*Initiative for the Development of Entrepreneurs in Agriculture*).

He is Of Counsel with the Law Offices of Kurt A. Wagner, a small international law firm with offices in Illinois and Austria. He and his wife Debbie and son Nathan live in Des Plaines, Illinois.

SPHINX® PUBLISHING'S STATE TITLES

Up-to-Date for Your State

California Titles

CA Power of Attorney Handbook (2E)	$18.95
How to File for Divorce in CA (4E)	$26.95
How to Probate & Settle an Estate in CA	$26.95
How to Start a Business in CA (2E)	$21.95
How to Win in Small Claims Court in CA (2E)	$18.95
The Landlord's Legal Guide in CA	$24.95
Make Your Own CA Will	$18.95
Tenants' Rights in CA	$21.95

Florida Titles

Child Custody, Visitation and Support in FL	$26.95
How to File for Divorce in FL (7E)	$26.95
How to Form a Corporation in FL (6E)	$24.95
How to Form a Limited Liability Co. in FL (2E)	$24.95
How to Form a Partnership in FL	$22.95
How to Make a FL Will (6E)	$16.95
How to Probate and Settle an Estate in FL (5E)	$26.95
How to Start a Business in FL (7E)	$21.95
How to Win in Small Claims Court in FL (7E)	$18.95
Land Trusts in Florida (6E)	$29.95
Landlords' Rights and Duties in FL (9E)	$22.95

Georgia Titles

How to File for Divorce in GA (5E)	$21.95
How to Make a GA Will (4E)	$21.95
How to Start a Business in Georgia (3E)	$21.95

Illinois Titles

Child Custody, Visitation and Support in IL	$24.95
How to File for Divorce in IL (3E)	$24.95
How to Make an IL Will (3E)	$16.95
How to Start a Business in IL (3E)	$21.95
The Landlord's Legal Guide in IL	$24.95

Maryland, Virginia and the District of Columbia

How to File for Divorce in MD, VA and DC	$28.95
How to Start a Business in MD, VA or DC	$21.95

Massachusetts Titles

How to Form a Corporation in MA	$24.95
How to Make a MA Will (2E)	$16.95
How to Start a Business in MA (3E)	$21.95
The Landlord's Legal Guide in MA	$24.95

Michigan Titles

How to File for Divorce in MI (3E)	$24.95
How to Make a MI Will (3E)	$16.95
How to Start a Business in MI (3E)	$18.95

Minnesota Titles

How to File for Divorce in MN	$21.95
How to Form a Corporation in MN	$24.95
How to Make a MN Will (2E)	$16.95

New Jersey Titles

How to File for Divorce in NJ	$24.95

New York Titles

Child Custody, Visitation and Support in NY	$26.95
File for Divorce in NY	$26.95
How to Form a Corporation in NY (2E)	$24.95
How to Make a NY Will (2E)	$16.95
How to Start a Business in NY (2E)	$18.95
How to Win in Small Claims Court in NY (2E)	$18.95
Landlords' Legal Guide in NY	$24.95
New York Power of Attorney Handbook	$19.95
Tenants' Rights in NY	$21.95

North Carolina and South Carolina Titles

How to File for Divorce in NC (3E)	$22.95
How to Make a NC Will (3E)	$16.95
How to Start a Business in NC or SC	$24.95
Landlords' Rights & Duties in NC	$21.95

Ohio Titles

How to File for Divorce in OH (2E)	$24.95
How to Form a Corporation in OH	$24.95
How to Make an OH Will	$16.95

Pennsylvania Titles

Child Custody, Visitation and Support in PA	$26.95
How to File for Divorce in PA (3E)	$26.95
How to Form a Croporation in PA	$24.95
How to Make a PA Will (2E)	$16.95
How to Start a Business in PA (3E)	$21.95
The Landlord's Legal Guide in PA	$24.95

Texas Titles

Child Custody, Visitation and Support in TX	$22.95
How to File for Divorce in TX (3E)	$24.95
How to Form a Corporation in TX (2E)	$24.95
How to Make a TX Will (3E)	$16.95
How to Probate and Settle an Estate in TX (3E)	$26.95
How to Start a Business in TX (3E)	$18.95
How to Win in Small Claims Court in TX (2E)	$16.95
The Landlord's Legal Guide in TX	$24.95

SPHINX® PUBLISHING'S NATIONAL TITLES
Valid in All 50 States

LEGAL SURVIVAL IN BUSINESS

The Complete Book of Corporate Forms	$24.95
The Complete Patent Book	$26.95
Employees' Rights	$18.95
Employer's Rights	$24.95
The Entrepreneur's Internet Handbook	$21.95
The Entrepreneur's Legal Guide	$26.95
How to Form a Limited Liability Company (2E)	$24.95
How to Form a Nonprofit Corporation (2E)	$24.95
How to Form Your Own Corporation (4E)	$26.95
How to Form Your Own Partnership (2E)	$24.95
How to Register Your Own Copyright (4E)	$24.95
How to Register Your Own Trademark (3E)	$21.95
Incorporate in Delaware from Any State	$24.95
Incorporate in Nevada from Any State	$24.95
Most Valuable Business Legal Forms You'll Ever Need (3E)	$21.95
Profit from Intellectual Property	$28.95
Protect Your Patent	$24.95
The Small Business Owner's Guide to Bankruptcy	$21.95
Tax Smarts for Small Business	$21.95

LEGAL SURVIVAL IN COURT

Attorney Responsibilities & Client Rights	$19.95
Crime Victim's Guide to Justice (2E)	$21.95
Grandparents' Rights (3E)	$24.95
Help Your Lawyer Win Your Case (2E)	$14.95
Jurors' Rights (2E)	$12.95
Legal Research Made Easy (3E)	$21.95
Winning Your Personal Injury Claim (2E)	$24.95
Your Rights When You Owe Too Much	$16.95

LEGAL SURVIVAL IN REAL ESTATE

The Complete Kit to Selling Your Own Home	$18.95
Essential Guide to Real Estate Contracts (2E)	$18.95
Essential Guide to Real Estate Leases	$18.95
Homeowner's Rights	$19.95
How to Buy a Condominium or Townhome (2E)	$19.95
How to Buy Your First Home	$18.95
Working with Your Homeowners Association	$19.95

LEGAL SURVIVAL IN SPANISH

Cómo Hacer su Propio Testamento	$16.95
Cómo Restablecer su propio Crédito y Renegociar sus Deudas	$21.95
Cómo Solicitar su Propio Divorcio	$24.95
Guía de Inmigración a Estados Unidos (3E)	$24.95
Guía de Justicia para Víctimas del Crimen	$21.95

Guía Esencial para los Contratos de Arrendamiento de Bienes Raices	$22.9
Inmigración a los EE. UU. Paso a Paso	$22.9
Manual de Beneficios para el Seguro Social	$18.9
El Seguro Social Preguntas y Respuestas	$14.9

LEGAL SURVIVAL IN PERSONAL AFFAIRS

101 Complaint Letters That Get Results	$18.9
The 529 College Savings Plan (2E)	$18.9
The Antique and Art Collector's Legal Guide	$24.9
The Complete Legal Guide to Senior Care	$21.9
Credit Smart	$18.9
Family Limited Partnership	$26.9
Gay & Lesbian Rights	$26.9
How to File Your Own Bankruptcy (5E)	$21.9
How to File Your Own Divorce (5E)	$26.9
How to Make Your Own Simple Will (3E)	$18.9
How to Write Your Own Living Will (3E)	$18.9
How to Write Your Own Premarital Agreement (3E)	$24.9
Living Trusts and Other Ways to Avoid Probate (3E)	$24.9
Mastering the MBE	$16.9
Most Valuable Personal Legal Forms You'll Ever Need (2E)	$26.9
Neighbor v. Neighbor (2E)	$16.9
The Nanny and Domestic Help Legal Kit	$22.9
The Power of Attorney Handbook (4E)	$19.9
Repair Your Own Credit and Deal with Debt (2E)	$18.9
Quick Cash	$14.9
Sexual Harassment:Your Guide to Legal Action	$18.9
The Social Security Benefits Handbook (3E)	$18.9
Social Security Q&A	$12.9
Teen Rights	$22.9
Traveler's Rights	$21.9
Unmarried Parents' Rights (2E)	$19.9
U.S. Immigration and Citizenship Q&A	$16.9
U.S. Immigration Step by Step (2E)	$24.9
U.S.A. Immigration Guide (5E)	$26.9
The Visitation Handbook	$18.9
The Wills, Estate Planning and Trusts Legal Kit	&26.9
Win Your Unemployment Compensation Claim (2E)	$21.9
Your Right to Child Custody, Visitation and Support (2E)	$24.9

SPHINX® PUBLISHING ORDER FORM

	ISBN	Title	Retail	Qty	ISBN	Title	Retail
		SPHINX PUBLISHING NATIONAL TITLES		___	1-57248-104-8	How to Register Your Own Trademark (3E)	$21.95
___	1-57248-363-6	101 Complaint Letters That Get Results	$18.95	___	1-57248-233-8	How to Write Your Own Living Will (3E)	$18.95
___	1-57248-361-X	The 529 College Savings Plan (2E)	$18.95	___	1-57248-156-0	How to Write Your Own	$24.95
___	1-57248-349-0	The Antique and Art Collector's Legal Guide	$24.95			Premarital Agreement (3E)	
___	1-57248-347-4	Attroney Responsibilities & Client Rights	$19.95	___	1-57248-230-3	Incorporate in Delaware from Any State	$26.95
___	1-57248-148-X	Cómo Hacer su Propio Testamento	$16.95	___	1-57248-158-7	Incorporate in Nevada from Any State	$24.95
___	1-57248-226-5	Cómo Restablecer su propio Crédito y	$21.95	___	1-57248-250-8	Inmigración a los EE.UU. Paso a Paso	$22.95
		Renegociar sus Deudas		___	1-57071-333-2	Jurors' Rights (2E)	$12.95
___	1-57248-147-1	Cómo Solicitar su Propio Divorcio	$24.95	___	1-57248-223-0	Legal Research Made Easy (3E)	$21.95
___	1-57248-166-8	The Complete Book of Corporate Forms	$24.95	___	1-57248-165-X	Living Trusts and Other Ways to	$24.95
___	1-57248-353-9	The Complete Kit to Sellng Your Own Home	$18.95			Avoid Probate (3E)	
___	1-57248-229-X	The Complete Legal Guide to Senior Care	$21.95	___	1-57248-186-2	Manual de Beneficios para el Seguro Social	$18.95
___	1-57248-201-X	The Complete Patent Book	$26.95	___	1-57248-220-6	Mastering the MBE	$16.95
___	1-57248-369-5	Credit Smart	$18.95	___	1-57248-167-6	Most Val. Business Legal Forms	$21.95
___	1-57248-163-3	Crime Victim's Guide to Justice (2E)	$21.95			You'll Ever Need (3E)	
___	1-57248-367-9	Employees' Rights	$18.95	___	1-57248-360-1	Most Val. Personal Legal Forms	$26.95
___	1-57248-365-2	Employer's Rights	$24.95			You'll Ever Need (2E)	
___	1-57248-251-6	The Entrepreneur's Internet Handbook	$21.95	___	1-57248-098-X	The Nanny and Domestic Help Legal Kit	$22.95
___	1-57248-235-4	The Entrepreneur's Legal Guide	$26.95	___	1-57248-089-0	Neighbor v. Neighbor (2E)	$16.95
___	1-57248-346-6	Essential Guide to Real Estate Contracts (2E)	$18.95	___	1-57248-169-2	The Power of Attorney Handbook (4E)	$19.95
___	1-57248-160-9	Essential Guide to Real Estate Leases	$18.95	___	1-57248-332-6	Profit from Intellectual Property	$28.95
___	1-57248-254-0	Family Limited Partnership	$26.95	___	1-57248-329-6	Protect Your Patent	$24.95
___	1-57248-331-8	Gay & Lesbian Rights	$26.95	___	1-57248-385-7	Quick Cash	$14.95
___	1-57248-139-0	Grandparents' Rights (3E)	$24.95	___	1-57248-344-X	Repair Your Own Credit and Deal with Debt (2E)	$18.95
___	1-57248-188-9	Guía de Inmigración a Estados Unidos (3E)	$24.95	___	1-57248-350-4	El Seguro Social Preguntas y Respuestas	$14.95
___	1-57248-187-0	Guía de Justicia para Víctimas del Crimen	$21.95	___	1-57248-217-6	Sexual Harassment: Your Guide to Legal Action	$18.95
___	1-57248-253-2	Guía Esencial para los Contratos de	$22.95	___	1-57248-219-2	The Small Business Owner's Guide to Bankruptcy	$21.95
		Arrendamiento de Bienes Raices		___	1-57248-168-4	The Social Security Benefits Handbook (3E)	$18.95
___	1-57248-103-X	Help Your Lawyer Win Your Case (2E)	$14.95	___	1-57248-216-8	Social Security Q&A	$12.95
___	1-57248-334-2	Homeowner's Rights	$21.95	___	1-57248-221-4	Teen Rlghts	$22.95
___	1-57248-164-1	How to Buy a Condominium or Townhome (2E)	$19.95	___	1-57248-366-0	Tax Smarts for Small Business	$21.95
___	1-57248-328-8	How to Buy Your First Home	$18.95	___	1-57248-335-0	Traveler's Rights	$21.95
___	1-57248-191-9	How to File Your Own Bankruptcy (5E)	$21.95	___	1-57248-236-2	Unmarried Parents' Rights (2E)	$19.95
___	1-57248-343-1	How to File Your Own Divorce (5E)	$26.95	___	1-57248-362-8	U.S. Immigration and Citizenship Q&A	$16.95
___	1-57248-222-2	How to Form a Limited Liability Company (2E)	$24.95	___	1-57248-387-3	U.S. Immigration Step by Step (2E)	$24.95
___	1-57248-231-1	How to Form a Nonprofit Corporation (2E)	$24.95	___	1-57248-392-X	U.S.A. Immigration Guide (5E)	$26.95
___	1-57248-345-8	How to Form Your Own Corporation (4E)	$26.95	___	1-57248-192-7	The Visitation Handbook	$18.95
___	1-57248-224-9	How to Form Your Own Partnership (2E)	$24.95	___	1-57248-225-7	Win Your Unemployment	$21.95
___	1-57248-232-X	How to Make Your Own Simple Will (3E)	$18.95			Compensation Claim (2E)	
___	1-57248-200-1	How to Register Your Own Copyright (4E)	$24.95		**Form Continued on Following Page**		**SubTotal**___

Qty	ISBN	Title	Retail
_____	1-57248-330-X	The Wills, Estate Planning and Trusts Legal Kit	&26.95
_____	1-57248-138-2	Winning Your Personal Injury Claim (2E)	$24.95
_____	1-57248-333-4	Working with Your Homeowners Association	$19.95
_____	1-57248-162-5	Your Right to Child Custody, Visitation and Support (2E)	$24.95
_____	1-57248-157-9	Your Rights When You Owe Too Much	$16.95

CALIFORNIA TITLES

Qty	ISBN	Title	Retail
_____	1-57248-150-1	CA Power of Attorney Handbook (2E)	$18.95
_____	1-57248-337-7	How to File for Divorce in CA (4E)	$26.95
_____	1-57248-145-5	How to Probate and Settle an Estate in CA	$26.95
_____	1-57248-336-9	How to Start a Business in CA (2E)	$21.95
_____	1-57248-194-3	How to Win in Small Claims Court in CA (2E)	$18.95
_____	1-57248-246-X	Make Your Own CA Will	$18.95
_____	1-57248-196-X	The Landlord's Legal Guide in CA	$24.95
_____	1-57248-241-9	Tenants' Rights in CA	$21.95

FLORIDA TITLES

Qty	ISBN	Title	Retail
_____	1-57071-363-4	Florida Power of Attorney Handbook (2E)	$16.95
_____	1-57248-176-5	How to File for Divorce in FL (7E)	$26.95
_____	1-57248-356-3	How to Form a Corporation in FL (6E)	$24.95
_____	1-57248-203-6	How to Form a Limited Liability Co. in FL (2E)	$24.95
_____	1-57071-401-0	How to Form a Partnership in FL	$22.95
_____	1-57248-113-7	How to Make a FL Will (6E)	$16.95
_____	1-57248-088-2	How to Modify Your FL Divorce Judgment (4E)	$24.95
_____	1-57248-354-7	How to Probate and Settle an Estate in FL (5E)	$26.95
_____	1-57248-339-3	How to Start a Business in FL (7E)	$21.95
_____	1-57248-204-4	How to Win in Small Claims Court in FL (7E)	$18.95
_____	1-57248-202-8	Land Trusts in Florida (6E)	$29.95
_____	1-57248-338-5	Landlords' Rights and Duties in FL (9E)	$22.95

GEORGIA TITLES

Qty	ISBN	Title	Retail
_____	1-57248-340-7	How to File for Divorce in GA (5E)	$21.95
_____	1-57248-180-3	How to Make a GA Will (4E)	$21.95
_____	1-57248-341-5	How to Start a Business in Georgia (3E)	$21.95

ILLINOIS TITLES

Qty	ISBN	Title	Retail
_____	1-57248-244-3	Child Custody, Visitation, and Support in IL	$24.95
_____	1-57248-206-0	How to File for Divorce in IL (3E)	$24.95
_____	1-57248-170-6	How to Make an IL Will (3E)	$16.95
_____	1-57248-247-8	How to Start a Business in IL (3E)	$21.95
_____	1-57248-252-4	The Landlord's Legal Guide in IL	$24.95

MARYLAND, VIRGINIA AND THE DISTRICT OF COLUMBIA

Qty	ISBN	Title	Retail
_____	1-57248-240-0	How to File for Divorce in MD, VA and DC	$28.95
_____	1-57248-359-8	How to Start a Business in MD, VA or DC	$21.95

MASSACHUSETTS TITLES

Qty	ISBN	Title	Retail
_____	1-57248-128-5	How to File for Divorce in MA (3E)	$24.95
_____	1-57248-115-3	How to Form a Corporation in MA	$24.95
_____	1-57248-108-0	How to Make a MA Will (2E)	$16.95
_____	1-57248-248-6	How to Start a Business in MA (3E)	$21.95
_____	1-57248-209-5	The Landlord's Legal Guide in MA	$24.95

MICHIGAN TITLES

Qty	ISBN	Title	Retail
_____	1-57248-215-X	How to File for Divorce in MI (3E)	$24.95
_____	1-57248-182-X	How to Make a MI Will (3E)	$16.95
_____	1-57248-183-8	How to Start a Business in MI (3E)	$18.95

MINNESOTA TITLES

Qty	ISBN	Title	Ret
_____	1-57248-142-0	How to File for Divorce in MN	$21.9
_____	1-57248-179-X	How to Form a Corporation in MN	$24.9
_____	1-57248-178-1	How to Make a MN Will (2E)	$16.9

NEW JERSEY TITLES

Qty	ISBN	Title	Ret
_____	1-57248-239-7	How to File for Divorce in NJ	$24.9

NEW YORK TITLES

Qty	ISBN	Title	Ret
_____	1-57248-193-5	Child Custody, Visitation and Support in NY	$26.9
_____	1-57248-351-2	File for Divorce in NY	$26.
_____	1-57248-249-4	How to Form a Corporation in NY (2E)	$24.9
_____	1-57248-095-5	How to Make a NY Will (2E)	$16.9
_____	1-57248-199-4	How to Start a Business in NY (2E)	$18.
_____	1-57248-198-6	How to Win in Small Claims Court in NY (2E)	$18.
_____	1-57248-197-8	Landlords' Legal Guide in NY	$24.
_____	1-57071-188-7	New York Power of Attorney Handbook	$19.
_____	1-57248-122-6	Tenants' Rights in NY	$21.

NORTH CAROLINA AND SOUTH CAROLINA TITLES

Qty	ISBN	Title	Ret
_____	1-57248-185-4	How to File for Divorce in NC (3E)	$22.
_____	1-57248-129-3	How to Make a NC Will (3E)	$16.
_____	1-57248-371-7	How to Start a Business in NC or SC	$24.
_____	1-57248-091-2	Landlords' Rights & Duties in NC	$21.

NORTH CAROLINA AND SOUTH CAROLINA TITLES

Qty	ISBN	Title	Ret
_____	1-57248-371-7	How to Start a Business in NC or SC	$24.

OHIO TITLES

Qty	ISBN	Title	Ret
_____	1-57248-190-0	How to File for Divorce in OH (2E)	$24.
_____	1-57248-174-9	How to Form a Corporation in OH	$24.
_____	1-57248-173-0	How to Make an OH Will	$16.

PENNSYLVANIA TITLES

Qty	ISBN	Title	Ret
_____	1-57248-242-7	Child Custody, Visitation and Support in PA	$26.
_____	1-57248-211-7	How to File for Divorce in PA (3E)	$26.
_____	1-57248-358-X	How to Form a Croporation in PA	$24.
_____	1-57248-094-X	How to Make a PA Will (2E)	$16.
_____	1-57248-357-1	How to Start a Business in PA (3E)	$21.
_____	1-57248-245-1	The Landlord's Legal Guide in PA	$24.

TEXAS TITLES

Qty	ISBN	Title	Ret
_____	1-57248-171-4	Child Custody, Visitation, and Support in TX	$22.
_____	1-57248-172-2	How to File for Divorce in TX (3E)	$24.
_____	1-57248-114-5	How to Form a Corporation in TX (2E)	$24.
_____	1-57248-255-9	How to Make a TX Will (3E)	$16.
_____	1-57248-214-1	How to Probate and Settle an Estate in TX (3E)	$26.
_____	1-57248-228-1	How to Start a Business in TX (3E)	$18.
_____	1-57248-111-0	How to Win in Small Claims Court in TX (2E)	$16.
_____	1-57248-355-5	The Landlord's Legal Guide in TX	$24.

SubTotal This page _____

SubTotal previous page _____

Shipping— $5.00 for 1st book, $1.00 each additional _____

Illinois residents add 6.75% sales tax _____

Connecticut residents add 6.00% sales tax _____

Total _____

You Have Touched
So Many Hearts